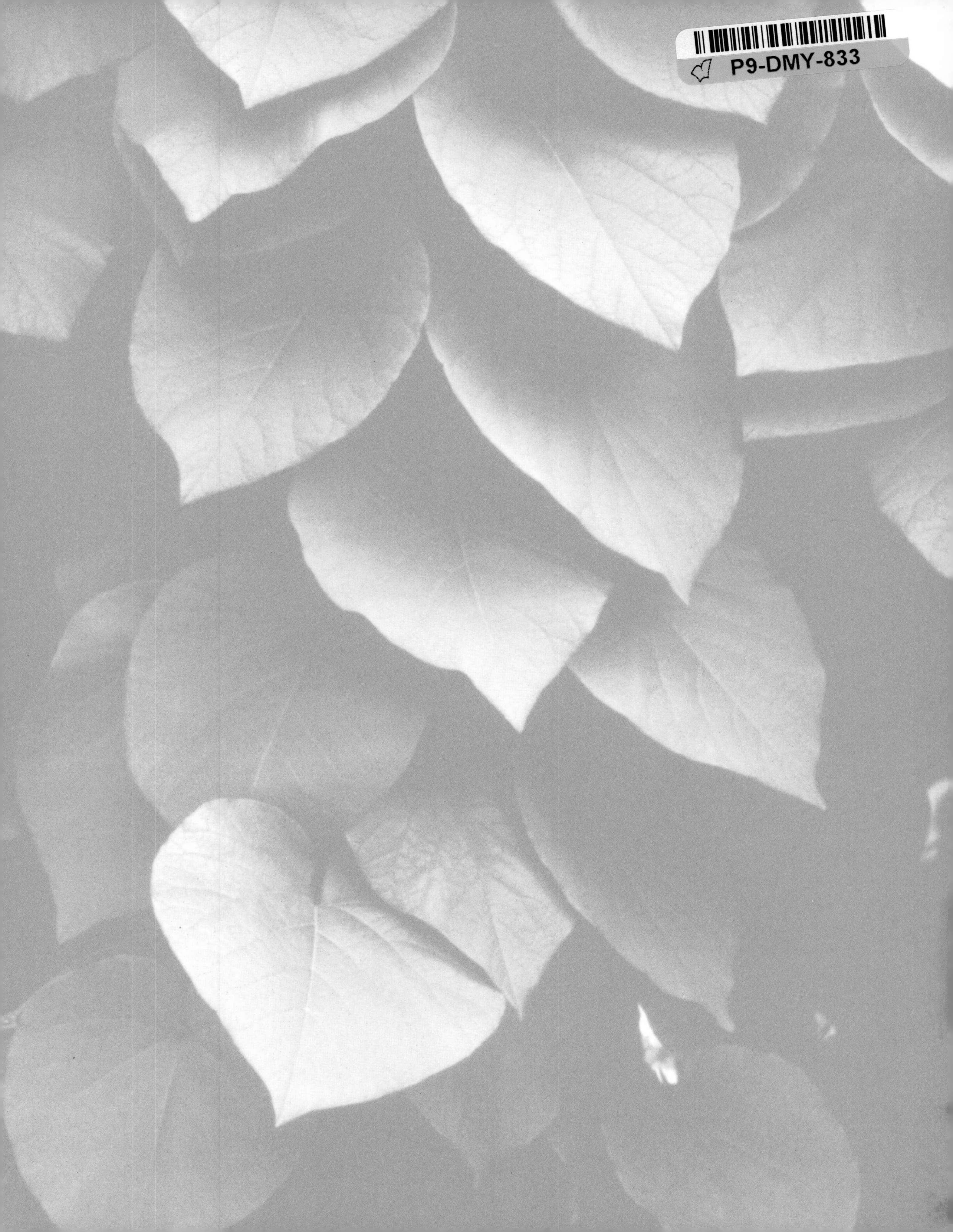

The Natural
Habitat Garden

THE NATURAL HABITAT GARDEN

KEN DRUSE

with MARGARET ROACH

PHOTOGRAPHS BY KEN DRUSE

DESIGN BY BARBARA PECK

Clarkson Potter/Publishers
New York

To America's nature writers, nature lovers, and all the

native-plant nursery owners and garden designers

who, against great odds, have held fast to finally see the

day when their efforts are recognized. These people have

devoted their careers to propagating and planting

wildflowers—never collecting them—so, although

the homes of native plants vanish, they will live

on in habitat gardens.

FIRST PAGE: *Anise hyssop,* Agastache foeniculum.
TITLE PAGE: *Northern California native flowers.*
RIGHT: *Taconic Falls in Ithaca, New York.*
OPPOSITE: Clematis ochroleuca, *leather flower.*
OVERLEAF: *A well-balanced pond in New England.*

COPYRIGHT © 1994 BY KEN DRUSE

Published by Clarkson N. Potter, Inc., 201 East 50th Street, New York,
New York 10022. Member of the Crown Publishing Group.

Random House, Inc. New York, Toronto, London, Sydney, Auckland.

CLARKSON N. POTTER, POTTER, and colophon are trademarks of
Clarkson N. Potter, Inc.

Manufactured in Japan

LIBRARY OF CONGRESS CATALOGING-IN-PUBLICATION DATA
Druse, Ken. The natural habitat garden / Ken Druse with Margaret
Roach. — 1st ed.
    Includes bibliographical references and index.
    1. Natural landscaping.   2. Habitat (Ecology)   I. Roach,
Margaret. II. Title.
SB439.D66 1994
635.9′51—dc20   93-12558
                                                      CIP

ISBN 0-517-58989-3

10 9 8 7 6 5 4 3 2 1

First Edition

ACKNOWLEDGMENTS

ENVIRONMENTALISTS WANT TO PRESERVE THE earth—natural habitat gardeners also want to replenish it.

The Natural Garden, published in 1989, presented an unpretentious approach to landscape design. *The Natural Shade Garden,* in 1992, relied a bit more on natives to help plantings reach self-sufficiency. The first book was for sun, the second for shade. *The Natural Habitat Garden,* on the other hand, is for the twenty-first century; and it may be controversial. Although it is a warning against uncontrolled consumption, it is not an indictment of conventional gardening—just a plea to give back to our environment some of the beauty and pleasure it has given us. This book will help to create niches, however small, that considered together can expand the realm of the indigenous plants and animals. I think the nature writer Joseph Wood Krutch's telling pun sums it up best, "A bird in the bush is worth two in the hand."

There are many people to thank for helping to promote this ideal and who contributed to bringing this book to light. At Clarkson Potter, I must thank my editor, friend, and promoter, Lauren Shakely; and Carol Southern, who was the first person to embrace this concept for publication; Art Director Howard Klein and this book's designer, Barbara Peck, whose contributions to the Natural Garden series are evident to everyone who shares these works. I'm proud to recognize others at Clarkson Potter: Andrea Connolly, Joan DeMayo, Jo Fagan, Phyllis Fleiss, Bruce Harris, Nancy Maloney, Barbara Marks, Mark McCauslin, Teresa Nicholas, Gail Shanks, Michelle Sidrane, Laurie Stark, Robin Strashun, Jane Treuhaft, Alberto Vitale, and Tina Zabriskie-Constable.

I'm proud to be associated with Helen Pratt, the agent for this work. Somehow she manages to remain true and sane throughout turbulent quests for common ground.

I would like to acknowledge horticultural and environmental advocates: Neil Diboll, Judith Stark, David Mahler, Judy Walther, Ken Moore and the organizers of the Cullowhee Native Plant Conference, Tovah Martin, Patti and Schellie Hagan, Charles Cresson, Suzanne Frutig Bales, Barbara Pryor and the staff and members of the New England Wildflower Society, Bob Zeleniak, John Trexler, Judy Zuk, Marco Polo Stufano, and Kim and Bruce Hawks. Helpful supporters: Marilyn Ratner, Patrick Smith, Miranda Genova, and Kristin Frederickson. Caring friends: George Waffle, Tom Dolle, Jim and Conni Cross.

I hope this new book will be as much of a source of pride to my parents, Helen and Harold Druse, as my first.

I would also like to thank Louis Bauer who is not only a devoted naturalist and a talented and tireless gardener but also an artist who has inspired me and helped me to improve every aspect of my work and life.

The contribution made by Margaret Roach to this book cannot be overstated—it can barely be expressed. She not only helped to write the text but also provided the discipline I needed to keep me on track when my train-of-thought derailed. (She would probably thank Taco Bell for her locomotion.) She is a brilliant environmentalist and writer and the greatest friend.

CONTENTS

PREFACE

WHEN I WROTE *THE NATURAL GARDEN* IN THE mid-1980s, I proposed that nature be the source of design. Now instead of just making gardens that resemble the earth, I want to enlarge the earth's diminished domain by growing native-plant gardens modeled on nature's original communities. I still believe that we need to go back to nature, but farther back—to the land as it was before development.

My previous book, *The Natural Shade Garden,* explored this strategy, emulating the woodland to create homes for shade-loving plants. But assembling plants from all corners of the world does not create a self-sufficient, ecologically appropriate community.

Evolution has produced a harmony that contrived gardens defy. Too often, man-made gardens counter the natural order of things. In the twenty-first century, the availability of water will have the greatest influence on gardening. The best way to garden without supplemental water is to welcome back indigenous vegetation.

As yet, I haven't ripped out my hostas and other collector plants. But the path I have taken since I began this book has certainly changed the way I look at them and has led me to pay attention to their place in the bigger ecological picture. I have also set out to find ways to apply my evolving views to gardening.

When people asked what I was working on during the last couple of years, I sometimes jokingly answered, "The Super-Natural Garden." What I meant was that the gardens I was seeing, the ones represented in this book, were more than just naturalistic. They attempt to simulate natural habitats. Each and every gardener whose work is included here discovered that once indigenous plants were brought back to the site, native birds, animals, and insects followed. It's no longer good enough to simply make it pretty, they have come to understand; it has to work, too.

I have always felt that the rhythm of the earth was my divinity, and researching *The Natural Habitat Garden* has certainly been a religious experience. With my colleague and friend Margaret Roach, I have traveled around the country, seeking instruction not just from nature's aesthetic side, but from the actual workings of the nation's dwindling reserve of wild places. We also sought out gardeners and gardens that were similarly inspired by the same functional models, America's habitats.

What we found, sometimes in very unlikely spots, was that a grass-roots movement—well, a grass-roots movement whose lawn has been dug up and replaced with natives—was quietly sweeping across the United States, one garden at a time.

An insightful landscape designer in Texas said it is reminiscent of the way the women's movement grew, and, although the comparison may seem grandiose, I think he's exactly right. It's happening all over the country, but not because of any central edict handed down from on high. It's happening simply because all these separate people sense, as I do, that habitat gardens are essential to the planet's future.

"Someday, they'll all come together to form a new order as influential as the Liberation movement," David Mahler, the visionary Texan, said.

I like to think of this book as the first public meeting place for many of these disconnected, but like-minded, advocate factions.

"A thing is right when it tends to preserve the integrity, stability and beauty of the biotic community," Aldo Leopold, father of the conservation movement, wrote in *A Sand County Almanac* in 1949.

Today, a garden is right when it does the very same thing. As a significant bonus, growing a natural habitat garden is also one of the most important things each of us can do to help restore a little order to a disordered world. Powerful stuff—and beautiful stuff, too.

KEN DRUSE
NEW YORK

"NATURE HAS NO HUMAN INHABITANT WHO APpreciates her," Henry David Thoreau wrote from his cabin at Walden Pond, Massachusetts, nearly 150 years ago. Imagine if he had lived to see what mankind hath wrought lately, particularly since the postwar building boom that created suburbia's antinatural landscape.

Today, we hear almost daily about the shrinking tropical rain forest, but somewhat frighteningly Americans seldom mention the deforesting of the Pacific Northwest, home of our very own rain forest

INTRODUCTION

and a repository of incredible biodiversity whose full extent has only been guessed.

Who in the course of a week gives even a minute to lamenting how little of the great American prairie still exists, or to the fact that 700,000 acres of this nation have been converted into parking lots in the short time since man, and his cars, have landed upon it? Meanwhile, the human population multiplies at a staggering rate: The current 5.4 billion tally is expected to reach 8.2 billion by the year 2020 and level off at 10 billion by the mid-twenty-first century. Forty percent of the world's population is now urbanized, triple the number since the 1950s, and development continues full-tilt.

A quarter of the earth's organisms may become extinct in the next thirty years—all gone in the moment of a single human generation—and many will vanish without a trace. Only 1.4 million plant and animal species have been recorded so far by scientists, who estimate that there are 10 million to 100 million out there. Not since the time of the dinosaurs, 65 million years ago, has there been such a mass extinction as the one a single species—humankind—

Walden Pond, RIGHT, *still remains an inspiration to countless environmentalists who revere the works of Henry David Thoreau. He wrote from his cabin,*

ABOVE, *re-created on the site. Only now, nearly 150 years after Thoreau preached respect for nature, are people beginning to pay attention and act to preserve the little bit that's left.*

has wreaked in the name of progress, convenience, and prosperity.

Gardening is indeed part of this scheme—or can be. If even a fraction of America's 38-million gardeners turned a quarter of their landscape into a re-wilded spot that recalls, at least roughly, its presettlement state, there would be a measurable impact. If every gardener gave just one tenth of an acre back, the instant net gain would be 3.8 million acres of native plants.

Even an imprecisely restored habitat has vastly more plant and animal diversity than America's ubiquitous turfgrass lawn (particularly a chemically treated one). The simplest wildflower meadow is more complex, more botanically varied, than a grass lawn, offering a long season of pollens, nectars, and finally seeds, along with nesting sites and shelter for all those creatures that used to live somewhere before we arrived.

Perhaps most important of all, a habitat-style garden of native plants welcomes the whole food chain —not just flowers, birds, and butterflies, but also a magnificent decaying tree stump teeming with life, ringed by otherworldly fluted layers of fungi. Rather than carting away decaying wood or mopping up puddles here, the natural habitat gardener rejoices at such happenings and the creatures who come in to bathe, drink, feed, or breed because of them. In the habitat garden, such "imperfections" are reasons for celebration—not a bout of obsessive tidying up. These spots are where the action is, and more effective than the most elegant birdbath or feeder money could buy. Never have the words *don't fight the site* held so much meaning. It is the habitat gardener's guiding principle.

Once nature's wrinkles come to be seen as opportunities, instead of problems to eliminate, a whole new flora and fauna can begin to unfold. And as the

TOP: *The northern cardinal, a familiar suburban resident, also frequents the desert when native vegetation is allowed to flourish.* ABOVE: *The tallgrass prairie is all but extinct, and although our Pacific Northwest rain forest,* OPPOSITE, *may not receive the media attention afforded the tropical jungles, its future is similarly imperiled.*

gardener gets the message about native plants—the effect they can have in making this all happen—things really start to take off.

Wonder of wonders, it happens on the very same territory that used to be near-monoculture—that lawn, that rose garden—a place that was barely hospitable to any but the "trash" birds, as opportunists like cowbirds, starlings, and the like are known. (Many animals feed on specific plants and accept no substitutes.) And with a little luck, the gardener himself will be drawn in by the small miracle unfolding in the yard, and increase the share of the property planted in this style. Before long, the next link in the chain is connected: Spurred to action by the new-found convictions, the habitat gardener begins to voice concern that local highways, parks, school-yards, and businesses start doing likewise, and even more potential habitat moves back into the pool.

More habitat, more biodiversity—the greater number of distinct species that can coexist.

"When you increase the area of a habitat ten-fold," says Edward O. Wilson, the noted Harvard biologist, "you double the number of species that can live there."

So as we enter what Dr. Wilson calls the critical bottleneck of the next fifty years, a time of exploding human population and shrinking biodiversity, we had each better think about our actions. We must act to save every species—from bacteria on up, scientists say, since even the little-studied, unseen world of microbial soil life-forms may prove to possess the key to global survival.

We must eliminate the use of potentially hazardous chemicals from all phases of our life, from house-cleaning to pest control in the garden. The toxic effects of herbicides, pesticides, and fungicides have been well documented in recent years, but chemical nitrogen fertilizers, too, greatly reduce the inhabita-bility of the soil and water they touch. Increasing soil life, not killing it, has to take top priority in our agendas, since the soil is the source of much life on earth.

Reduce, reuse, recycle—this time with a vengeance—and be particularly careful to conserve when water or energy is at stake. Compost, indoors with the help of earthworms, outdoors in a more traditional heap.

Grow a garden, but not just turfgrass lawn and hybrid tea roses. Create instead a natural habitat garden based on indigenous plant species that are appropriate to the precise site conditions and geographic location, not just to how cold or hot the area gets in an average year. In evaluating your site, take into consideration what would have been there and nearby presettlements working from researched models (in regional and local guides, old topographical maps, museums, and arboretums, for example) —before the bulldozers pulled in and put up a parking lot—not just what exists today.

This kind of leap forward in landscaping styles and plant selection can actually help offset the losses of habitat elsewhere on the planet. Plants and animals being forced out of their native range may find refuge in these little, privately created safety zones. Though the plight of global preservation efforts in the world's hotspots—zones targeted by scientists as being particularly diverse, and therefore urgently in need of protection—will continue to be more critical with every passing day, here is something else every gardener can do, in addition to supporting green organizations with donations.

Standing dead trees are homes for birds. Fallen logs support hosts of insects, mammals, mosses, ferns, tree seedlings, and perhaps a colony of fluted agatelike fungi, OPPOSITE, ABOVE. *Every bit of captured water is useful, and every bit of matter used. A rock crevice makes a convenient watering stop for birds,* BELOW.

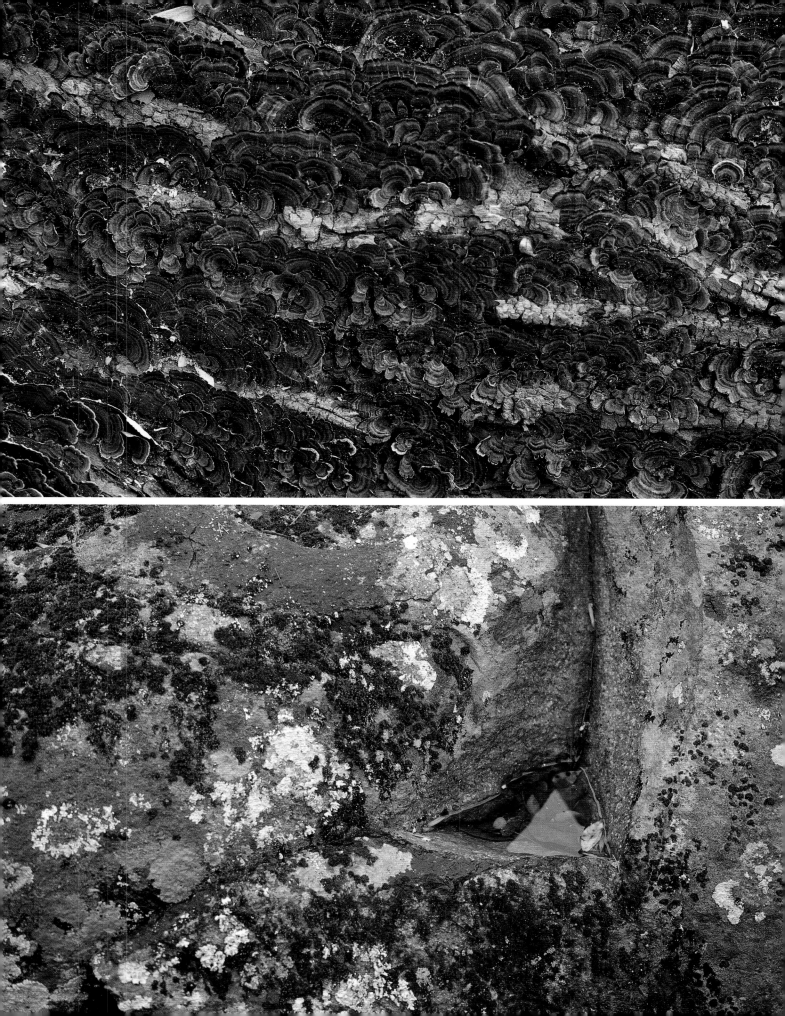

Never bring an invasive plant into the landscape. In 1935 the federal government planted 73 million seedlings of kudzu, BELOW (swallowing a tree), to control erosion along road cuts. This monster has covered and choked trees and fields, and has virtually swallowed the Southeast. Although it is somewhat controlled by harsh winters, it has been spotted in New York State. Japanese honeysuckle, Oriental bittersweet, multiflora rose, crown vetch, and autumn olive are devastating counterparts in the North, yet all of these plants are still sold as "quick problem-solvers" by less conscientious nurseries. Purple loosestrife, banned in a few states, causes millions of dollars in damage to crops and wildlife. In its native European habitat, it is controlled by indigenous insects. Allegedly "sterile" hybrids, able to contribute viable pollen, are still sold. These plants, along with countless diseases and pests, have been introduced intentionally or accidentally over the centuries.

Less is more in the home landscape of Ken Moore, assistant director of the University of North Carolina Botanical Garden at Chapel Hill, TOP RIGHT. He gardens by a process of elimination, editing out the plants he doesn't want. Often he hand-weeds or simply mows down some of the plants he wants to discourage. With an artful eye, and a great sense of humor, Moore, who is one of the founders of the Cullowhee (North Carolina) Native Plant Conference, arranged colorful gazing balls down an allée of grasses and forbs in November. RIGHT CENTER: Sources for native plants were rare; now places such as Native Texas Nurseries, which features silver cenizo (Leucophyllum candidum), are proliferating. Some of the native-plant seed sources for supplying the nurseries and home landscapes have come from unexpected areas—spared from development. One example was the rough of an old golf course; another the railroad easements of the Midwest, BOTTOM RIGHT.

IT'S NOT A JUNGLE OUT THERE

Few of us are willing to just let our property overgrow and go wild, and it's not the most sensible course in any case. Without intervention, the already-disturbed habitats we live in would simply head down the path to decline, with aggressive, opportunistic exotics increasing their domain over natives, and diversity succumbing to various versions of the "kudzu phenomenon," where an exotic plant overtakes whole regions of its new homeland.

"While nature herself is variable, disturbance is typically simplistic," Andropogon Associates, the Philadelphia-based ecological planning and design firm, wrote in a proposal on restoring the woodlands of New York's Central Park. "When disturbance is uncontrolled, deterioration usually accelerates and a once-rich site steadily diminishes in diversity, value, and interest. . . . Once disturbance is controlled," the report added, "the landscape will be far more able to control itself."

Although there is disagreement on how to manage and restore land, I believe the same hand that moved to hurt it can now help it to heal.

Instead of just letting things go, the habitat gardener may selectively handweed or mow each year at the appropriate time. Sometimes controlled burning can scarify hard-to-germinate seeds, remove layers of built-up debris that are hampering the growth of desirables, and otherwise get things moving (more on the powerful, natural tool of fire in the section on grasslands). Though you might guess it would be to the contrary, land grazed by herds of livestock on a sensible schedule may actually fare better over time in retaining some of its original diverse character than similar tracts that are fenced off—supposedly "protected"—and allowed to overgrow.

Friendly interventions like these help rekindle a dormant plant community whose seeds and other vestiges may still be hidden in the soil. Or in the worst cases, where nothing remains, not even the original topsoil, the habitat gardener can replant at least a symbolic version of the scene long vanished.

In the long run, a habitat-style garden will be easier to maintain once established than its more conventionally designed counterparts, but in the beginning, this approach is not low-maintenance. As landscape architect Gary Smith of the University of Delaware, a proponent of native landscapes, reminds us, a garden is a relationship between two living things, garden and gardener. "And how many no-maintenance relationships have you had in your life?" he quips.

Likewise, you need not cast out hostas, or alpines, or your favorite collector plants, so long as they do not have invasive, aggressive habits or impact negatively on the environment.

"Nature has a place for the wild clematis as well as for the cabbage," Thoreau wrote in his famous essay "Walking," though today, with things so far off-balance, he would probably reverse the emphasis between the indigenous plant and the introduced. "The matrix needs to be native to support the biodiversity we need to survive," Gary Smith concurs. Natural habitat garden design has a much bigger picture in mind than the confines of a bed or border.

Most homeowners, even those with just weekend homes, have at least a patch of lawn that would serve the planet and the place better as a prairie, or a wet sump that could begin to support wetland plant species if cultivated as such. Instead of struggling against nature in the arid American Southwest in order to install a lawn or herbaceous border, the natural habitat gardener can surrender aboveground sprinklers that waste money and water and create a home landscape that revels in the beauty of the desert.

WHAT'S IN IT FOR YOU

Making the commitment to garden in the habitat style is enriching, both for the gardener's life and for the future of the planet. One recent study in the Southwest, for example, showed that vegetation is the single most important factor in attracting birds, and that the greater the presence of native vegetation, the larger the population of native birds.

In some cases, these relationships are so strong that one cannot exist without the other. Survival of monarch butterflies depends on their being unpalatable to birds because of the toxins they ingest from certain milkweeds. Now that *Asclepias sylvaniaii* is disappearing, butterflies munch other, more available milkweed species, thus getting less predation protection per mouthful, increasing their risk of extinction.

Traditionally, butterfly bush (*Buddleia* spp., from China) and fuchsias (Central and South America and New Zealand) have been planted to attract butterflies to the garden. Yet native North American flora such as butterfly weed (*Asclepias* spp.), columbine, coneflowers, and penstemons are only a few of many enticing candidates that might make the difference in whether a species endures, at least in the immediate locale. In the natural habitat garden, spring is marked not by the emergence of crocuses (natives of Asia and Europe) but by skunk cabbages and shooting star (*Dodecatheon* spp.).

Hundreds of years ago, the New World's flora were first imported to Europe and treated as the finest garden treasures. Now we are finally discovering them ourselves, learning from this new landscape an awareness of our surroundings—dare I say roots?—as we can from no other garden. It teaches lessons of interdependence of species, wisdom man has lost living in his high-tech ivory tower. Americans spend only 5 percent of their time outdoors.

As I mentioned, the home habitat garden is also a place to grow and preserve plants that are threatened in the native ranges, though this good-doing does not condone the collection of plant specimens from the wild for use in the home landscape. Only nursery-propagated plants, or those acquired from a native-plant society or plant-rescue operation undertaken by a legitimate environmental group, are fair game. To plunder another habitat in the name of growing your own is unthinkable.

LETTING GO

"What unthinking people call design in nature is simply the reflection of our inevitable anthropomorphism," America's greatest nature writer, John Burroughs, wrote in 1920. "Whatever they can use, they think was designed for that purpose—the air to breathe, the water to drink, the soil to plant. It is as if they thought that notch in the mountains was made for the road to pass over. . . ."

Certainly such a voracious, me-first approach as the one man has taken in "developing" the land cannot continue, not even on the level of a single suburban lot. The challenge is to imagine the home landscape of the future.

"I'm not sure what the New American Garden is," says Darrel G. Morrison, dean of the School of Environmental Design at the University of Georgia, Athens, and a leading force in the native-plant move-

PRECEDING PAGES, LEFT: *In the Southwest, a spiny teddy-bear cholla* (Opuntia bigelovii) *makes a fortified nesting site for a cactus wren whose tough feet aren't bothered by the needles.* RIGHT: *The red admiral butterfly, found throughout the United States, sips nectar from one of its favorite plants, purple coneflower* (Echinacea purpurea). OPPOSITE: *Evelyn Adams has nurtured a glade garden of* Trillium grandiflorum *for fifty years. She hasn't intentionally practiced conservation through propagation; this is just the way "God gardens."*

ment. "But I am at least sure that it should be made of American plants." Gary Smith of the University of Delaware says the New American Garden is about letting the land speak its mind to you, about you listening. "You can't stamp [a style] on the place," he says. "You let the mystery reveal itself." For me, the New American Garden is one that respects the original archetype of the site and surrounding region, and continues to evolve over time. A living organism, it can't be trucked in and installed in time for tomorrow's tea party.

As soon as I started photographing gardens created in the habitat style—the ones I discovered in the process of producing this book—I began looking at every garden differently.

The works-in-progress contained in this book now form my new point of reference, the knowledge that I draw upon when thinking about how to design a sensible contemporary landscape in my next garden, or helping someone else to plan theirs. I call them works-in-progress because creating any garden takes

time, and this is even more relevant when you are working at more than a single border.

The gardeners behind the gardens—Neil Diboll burning his lawn to coax a prairie into life in Wisconsin; Evelyn Adams nurturing a glade of trilliums over a lifetime in Massachusetts; Dick Lighty selecting dwarf asters and goldenrods or shrub dogwoods with striking variegation on the Delaware-Pennsylvania border, and helping get them into the nursery trade, and all the rest—they are my new teachers, and my new heroes, pioneers of the new American landscape. I think as you turn the coming pages, they will become your inspirations, too.

IN THE BEGINNING

In *The Natural Garden,* I suggested thinking of the average home landscape as different areas that addressed the needs of the people who used the place. The natural habitat encompasses not just the needs of human beings but of plants and animals.

We have to devise new ways to get into the landscape: mowed paths, OPPOSITE; *viewing platforms,* ABOVE; *boardwalks,* RIGHT, *for instance one at Tower Hill Botanic Garden; and even treehouses,* TOP, *such as Carter and Suzanne Bales's elaborate retreat.*

The inner area of the homesite is still the high-traffic area with easy access to the house, a place for entertaining, for example, usually covered in a hard surface for utility. The outer area remains the zone with the lowest-maintenance, longest-lasting plants and also serves as a screen from the surrounding properties, if desired. The in-between area continues to house whatever suits the gardener's interests, but because the habitat gardener's focus has evolved, this area has undergone substantial change.

Now, the pavement of the inner area (a place for a dining set or a chaise, for instance) is chosen for environmental soundness, not looks alone. I have always recommended that it appear appropriate—that is, granite sets for a rocky area of New England, for example—but now it must really work, too, for the good of the site. Soil beneath a slab of concrete or asphalt just doesn't support much in the way of life, whereas individual stones or bricks actually form a favorite hiding place for soil-dwellers, and many plants like to tuck their roots underneath into the trapped pockets of moisture and grow mightily out of the cracks. In any paved area, water must be able to percolate downward, meaning that mortared joints are less desirable than sand or soil.

Raised decking makes a good choice for the hardscape of the inner area, both because it leaves the soil below unstressed and because it gives humans a lift —up high, where they can really look out into the habitat beyond, and enjoy the sights. If the in-

between area is to be in meadow, for instance, or wetland, or some other hard-to-traverse planting, a boardwalk extending from the deck through it invites participation without trampling. Viewing towers, boardwalks, platforms—these are all important additions to the habitat garden. At the very least, a mown path wide enough to accommodate two people side by side should be figured into the plan, though its precise course can vary from year to year.

The outer area should be as wild as possible. Give special thought to creating cover for birds, who on windy winter days will particularly appreciate an evergreen perching place (*Juniperus virginiana,* red cedar, is a favorite in many regions of the country).

Brushy edge areas offer protection from predators as well as nesting sites for many species; plan to make them edible as well as secure. Native plants like raspberry relatives (*Rubus* spp.), elderberry (*Sambucus* spp.), holly (*Ilex* spp.), native roses (including *Rosa palustris, R. virginiana, R. carolina, R. setigera*), black cherry (*Prunus serotina*), hawthorn (*Crataegus* spp.), cranberrybush (*Viburnum* spp.), blueberries (*Vaccinium* spp.), dogwood (*Cornus* spp.), spicebush (*Lindera benzoin*), red chokeberry (*Aronia arbutifolia*), noninvasive honeysuckle, such as *Lonicera sempervirens,*

Many plants are for the birds. ABOVE, LEFT TO RIGHT: *Swamp rose* (Rosa palustris) *will have nutritious hips. Eastern baccharis* (Baccharis halimifolia), *a wild seaside shrub, bears fuzzy white puffs called achenes attached to dry fruits containing a single seed. Elderberry* (Sambucus canadensis) *grows in waste places.*

sumac (*Rhus* spp.), baccharis (*Baccharis halimifolia*), cactus (*Opuntia* and *Ferocactus,* among others), ceanothus (*Ceanothus* spp.), and manzanita (*Arctostaphylos* spp.) are just a sampling of the many indigenous possibilities to tangle together.

Use your imagination to design blends of plants that weave into what I call biohedges—intermediate-height mixed plantings that serve multiple purposes to encourage, protect, and feed wildlife.

In this outer area, let a dead tree stand—remember, this is not a loss, but a cause for celebration, an offering from nature—unless it endangers people or property. In such cases, remove unwieldy limbs and top the tree if its uppermost portion is badly decayed, but leave as much of the trunk standing as possible—it's still a good place to raise a family. Leave removed portions of the trunk on the ground to decay in place, and use discarded twigs and branches to form a brush pile, a favorite home for numerous animal species.

The outer area doesn't have to be thought of as existing along the back, or fringe, of the property, either. It could be developed along the front and sides, too, so that the house is enclosed in its own cozy little sanctuary. If noise is a problem, a berm of soil developed as a mediating element between the home and the street is a possibility. It needn't be the landscapers' pile of dirt—dotted with spots of juniper. The berm itself can be another whole habitat, since its soil composition and terrain may differ from the rest of the property.

The in-between area, which in the past might have contained a mix of lawn and ornamental islands or borders of exotic perennials, for instance, is now the principal area of interactive habitat—where you and the other garden residents, both plants and animals, will come into closest contact. Ideally, the lawn is gone or reduced even further in favor of some more diverse planting, specifically natives, as in the outer area. In the best of scenarios, plant collections (like that perennial garden) may be modified to reflect the gardener's increased awareness of native plants.

Collections are probably afforded less space than before, in favor of plantings that give more to the big picture ecologically. Where vegetable or "collection gardens" remain, though, they need to be corralled by a fence or stone wall, or some other feature that sets them apart from the looser native landscape. A water element, which in the natural garden may have been simply a small garden pool, may receive greater emphasis in the habitat garden, where 15 percent of the total landscape should be planned as some kind of wetland—pond, bog, wet meadow, stream, or at the very least a significant garden pool. Even in the desert, where 15 percent would be too much, some consistently available source of water is welcome.

ABOVE, LEFT TO RIGHT: *American cranberry bush* (Viburnum trilobum), *one of the birds' favorites; the spikenard* (Aralia racemosa); *many cacti have fleshy fruits, such as prickly pear* (Opuntia rufida). *Caution: Do not eat any plant with which you are not familiar!*

The plantings around the house can do more than visually anchor it to the ground. Instead of plants that will soon outgrow their spots and require perpetual pruning, there are others that can participate in a landscape repertory company, playing more than one role at a time. Gray dogwood, for instance, is a highly ornamental but little-used shrub whose beautiful fruit birds adore; American viburnum species provide showy blooms plus wildlife food. Oregon holly grape (*Mahonia aquifolium*) is an evergreen with desirable fruits. Besides fruit, blueberries and deciduous hollies boast great fall foliage color. Many more species specific to particular habitats are mentioned in the chapters following.

IDENTIFYING YOUR HABITAT

GRASSLANDS are areas dominated by herbaceous plants like grasses and forbs; a prairie is a grassland, and so are plains and meadows and even many old fields.

WOODLANDS are those where woody plants, particularly trees, have the upper hand, which means that shade must be contended with all or part of the year.

WETLANDS are literally wet at least part of the time. Water controls what lives in this environment.

Absence of water is what makes DRYLANDS what they are. In these areas of low precipitation, and frequently high heat as well, all life-forms learn to make every drop of water count.

In each of these general habitats there is overlap—meadow-style plantings can be found in both wetlands and grasslands, for instance, since some prairie and meadow plants prefer wet soils and some do not.

A habitat does not obey the arbitrary man-made county lines or boundaries between your neighbor's home and your own. Habitats are living systems

Consider parts of your homesite in terms of general habitats, OPPOSITE, TOP TO BOTTOM: *grassland; woodland; wetland; and dryland. There are tiny subsystems called niches within these habitats. For instance, a shaded rock at Jennings Preserve in western Pennsylvania,* RIGHT, *is home to mosses, ferns, and* Clintonia umbellulata *(in flower).*

with many subsystems called niches—a pocket of rock outcropping within a woodland, for instance, is a niche. Habitats blend into one another regularly, and their boundaries also ebb and flow according to vagaries like weather. The tallgrass prairie recedes in times of prolonged drought, and the intermediate-height mixed-grass prairie steps into its place.

Start identifying your habitat by paging through this book to see what looks familiar, and by reading locally appropriate field guides. Since most of us in America live and garden in disturbed habitats, areas whose original character has long since given way to man's physical domination, the process may take some detective work. Armed with your notes, identify the oldest trees near your property, particularly native ones as clues to its presettlement character.

In the absence of such telltale landmarks, examine written records, such as county maps at the hall of records that indicate presettlement vegetation. If a group like The Nature Conservancy (see the "Source Guide" for addresses of native-plant societies and organizations) has protected some land nearby, it may provide clues to what used to grow where only your lawn does today.

Sometimes, the clues to what habitat is most appropriate come serendipitously, the way they did when P. Clifford Miller, a landscape designer in Lake Forest, Illinois, saw a dead fox squirrel in the road near a client's home. Miller knew that the fox squirrel was indigenous to savannas, an all-but-eliminated American grassland with sparse trees. Miller uses such animal indicators, along with other tools, such as the plants that grow along the nearby railroad

Within the habitat categories are smaller divisions called plant communities. An example lies among huge marble outcroppings at Bartholomew's Cobble, OPPOSITE, *in the Massachusetts Berkshires. This specific woodland is dominated by Canadian hemlock (Tsuga canadensis) over mosses, ferns, and pure white stone,* ABOVE.

easements, to help solve the puzzle of what plant communities and habitat styles would be most appropriate for the site. Animal-indicator tips are included in the best field guides, so don't overlook the opportunity they may provide.

A NEW WAY OF SEEING

It takes a sophisticated eye combined with a developed consciousness to find the beauty in the golden brown grasses of fall, or to accept that sometimes the stereotypical, brilliant succession of color we have always thought of as a "garden" simply isn't going to happen all the time. This new kind of garden requires an enduring sense of stewardship, so that the "huns"—as landscape restoration specialists Andropogon Associates, of Philadelphia, call those hungry exotics waiting to take over if permitted—never get their opportunity. Habitat gardeners think long-term —like forever. They start to think that way because evolution over time is the natural order of things. The natural habitat gardener can pass on the legacy by asking estate executors to use life insurance proceeds to remove potentially invasive plants and maintain the property with thoughtfulness toward the environment.

In nature, there is no truly independent action without impact.

NATIVE OR INDIGENOUS?

What is a locally appropriate plant? Purists suggest that we must seek out not just native plants from our region, but locally specific, or indigenous, species to help preserve the genetic integrity of the immediate local plant community. Grow species native to within fifty miles of your site, they recommend. If this sounds right to you, then subscribe to their fundamentalist ethic; you will be in good company among some prominent botanists and environmentalists.

Other scientists and native-plant experts, including David K. Northington, director of the National Wildflower Research Center, say such a tight interpretation of "native" is just too restrictive. Neil Diboll, an ecologist and owner of Prairie Nursery in Wisconsin, stresses, as does Northington, the sometimes-overlooked fact that it is normal for plants to undergo large-scale migrations over time. "People are biased toward animals migrating, but against plants doing so," says Diboll.

It is well documented geologically that plant communities migrate according to climatic conditions as minor as an extended drought or as dramatic as an ice age. Other natural forces including wind, birds, and other animals are also responsible for moving plants, usually in the form of seed, beyond their "normal" boundaries.

Here's what might happen if you order seeds or plants from one region to grow in another, says Northington: Seeds of a Georgia strain of rudbeckia (black-eyed Susan) for instance, accustomed to early springs in the warm South, might start to grow too early if planted by a gardener in Wisconsin. The reverse—trying a Wisconsin-grown species in Georgia—probably wouldn't be as difficult, and in either case you might succeed. So what's so awful, so dangerous about that? Probably nothing in the rudbeckia example, but a worse scenario, he explains, is that in some cases the local species and the imported species might cross and create a hybrid with greater vigor than either parent. This new generation might eventually outperform each parent until it disappears, forcing an extirpation (when a species vanishes from a particular area), or even an extinction —possible but rare.

Since most native-plant gardens don't even put their roots down into native soil, thanks to the bulldozers that carted it all away and sold it, I think we can be a little more flexible than the fifty-mile rule, too. Adhere to wider regional models, and patronize native-plant nurseries as close to home as possible that specialize in the plants of your region.

Many reference books call plants in wild places "wildflowers." But are these plants truly indigenous or are they naturalized—aliens that spread? The nearby fields of natives that explode with color are the inspirations for The National Wildflower Research Center, founded by Lady Bird Johnson in Austin, Texas.

ALL IN A NAME

A "genus" is a group of related species, i.e., the first word in a Latin name. A "species" (abbreviated "spp.") includes like individuals that can breed with each other. A "subspecies" is a division of plants that differ in small ways from the species and are usually found in specific populations and places. In horticulture, a "variety" is a group within a species that has small differences from the rest of the members. A plant known only in cultivation that may have been selected from a naturally occurring variety and propagated for garden use is a cultivated variety or "cultivar." A "hybrid" results from the cross-fertilization of two species, subspecies, or varieties.

Some of the more disease- and insect-resistant, more or less compact, or interesting plants for future habitat gardens are cultivars. For instance, in the genus *Echinacea,* there are a few versions of the species *purpurea,* the purple coneflower. These have white flowers: *E.p.* 'Alba' and *E.p.* 'White Swan'—white purple coneflowers. Another example occurred around the turn of the last century. A spectacular version of the rather unassuming native shrub *Hydrangea arborescens* was discovered in a garden by two women in Union County and transplanted to Anna, Illinois, in 1910. Unlike its single-flowered predecessor, this sturdy one had voluptuous double flowers. In 1960, it was introduced to gardeners. Now it is known as the familiar cultivar 'Annabelle'.

WILDFLOWER OR WEED?

The country roadside in many regions in summertime is positively captivating: waves of Queen Anne's lace (*Daucus carota*) and blue chicory (*Cichorium intybus*), or embankments sweet with the perfume of thousands of tiny white roses (*Rosa multiflora*). Wildflowers, right? Not so, at least not by the standards of the National Wildflower Research Center.

NWRC would like gardeners to regard all native plants—whether trillium or little bluestem grass or a dogwood tree—as wildflowers, and to use naturalized plants to refer to roadside aliens like chicory and Queen Anne's lace.

Some foreign plants just settle into American soil for a time, then fade away; others spread slowly in their new land; and a third class really gets going—the kudzu types, or purple loosestrifes. As even a short visit by a nonnative can upset the balance of the community enough to cause extirpation or even extinction of a native plant, all of these invasions are undesirable.

NWRC wants gardeners to understand the concept of environmental weeds, like the multiflora rose, that have a deleterious impact on the environment. The mockingbirds may love the rose, but the birds who enjoyed its predecessors, the native raspberry (*Rubus* spp.) and seed-producing herbaceous plants, have disappeared. Put simply, two plants can't share the very same spot. That, in a sentence, is perhaps the most compelling case of all for natives.

ABOVE: *"Naturalized" wildings, or "weeds," daylilies, the common buttercup, and Queen Anne's lace.*
CLOCKWISE FROM BELOW: *A propagated selection of* Hydrangea arborescens *called 'Annabelle'; the cultivar of purple coneflower* (Echinacea purpurea) *'White Swan'; a floriferous form of New England aster* (Aster novae-angliae).

To become a new American landscaper, whether professional or hobbyist, the gardener needs to stretch beyond the current suburban models for inspiration and to stop mimicking the intricate imposing borders of English garden books.

We must start gardening and landscaping according to habitat. This book is organized into general habitat categories called grasslands, drylands, wetlands, and woodlands. If you live in a desert, you probably know it; in fact, you may have moved to your current home because it was in an arid zone and you wanted to enjoy its dry climate. Woodlands are identifiable too, particularly if you're in the middle of one. But some of America's habitats are a lot less obvious, and even among what we loosely call deserts there is great variability: high deserts and low ones, for instance, with considerable differences of temperature extremes and annual precipitation that alter the plant palette.

More important, when you look beyond the habitat level, the differences really begin to stand out. Scientists have identified more than one hundred plant communities in America, named according to the dominant species and inhabited by plants similarly adapted to the local climate, soil type, and other factors, including their ability to grow successfully together as a group. A sedge meadow is an example of a plant community; so is a pine-oak woodland, or a tallgrass prairie.

Botanists, conservationists, and experts in landscape restoration frequently think in terms of these

It may take a more sophisticated sensibility to find beauty in the amber waves of grasses in late summer, LEFT. OPPOSITE: *No plant is an island. Plants grow in societal groups called plant communities, such as these dryland citizens: a brushy agave surrounded by tall ocotillo* (Fouquieria splendens) *and opuntia cacti.*

What a wealth we would have if our prairie roads could

be lined with this rich carpet of colors, miles of flowers

reflecting their colors in the sky above, or millions of sungods

(sunflowers) in the strong prairie breeze nodding their

heads to the sun that had given them their golden hue.

But perhaps that is too much to hope for,

as man seems unappreciative of these gifts.

~ JENS JENSEN

THE AFTERNOON HAD A SENSE OF DISCOVERY about it, as if we were witnessing something no one had ever seen before—hardly the case, but definitely the feeling. Walking through the three-thousand-year-old prairie at the University of Wisconsin–Madison was not unlike coming face-to-face with a woolly mammoth or some other creature thought to be extinct, a compelling organism sadly lost forever —or nearly lost, in the prairie's case.

The three-thousand-year-old prairie at the University of Wisconsin–Madison, RIGHT, *hosts tall prairie dock* (Silphium terebinthinaceum) *and the white spikes of Culver's root* (Veronicastrum virginicum). ABOVE: *A goldfinch gleans tasty seeds.*

Although not as colorful as the rest of the university's extensive layout of restored and re-created prairies, this ecological elder was the one we had traveled to see. While other visitors on the same hot, cloudless August afternoon were unable to take their eyes off the mass of lavender bergamot (*Monarda fistulosa*) and yellow coneflower (*Ratibida pinnata*) in adjacent, man-made plantings by the parking lot, Margaret and I, like a pair of pilgrims at an ancient shrine, headed for the relict area—the "persistent remnant of an otherwise extinct flora or fauna or kind of organism," as the dictionary explains the term.

It was a far cry from today's trendy wildflower meadow plantings, but what this rugged survivor before us lacked in flash appeal it more than made up for in soul.

With each footstep along its trails and firelanes (bare strips that serve to control the burning performed in spring to stimulate new growth and check invasion by woody species), we knew we were treading on soil fertile enough to have produced several millennia of plant life. In turn, the prairie flora before us had given life, in the form of pollen, nectar, seed, and, of course, those nutrient-rich grass blades and leaves, to countless generations of animal creatures whose presence could almost be felt.

We also knew that the same deep, rich soil underfoot has proved to be the prairie's undoing.

Once, America's grasslands counted half a million Native Americans, 25 million bison, and 48 million prairie dogs (other estimates range upward to several billion prairie dogs) among the life-forms they supported. Today, many of these indigenous citizens are nearly extinct, and the habitat-turned-heartland instead feeds one in every twelve of the planet's human inhabitants. Where once three hundred or more predominantly herbaceous native species of plants coexisted, digging down their soil-improving roots into the ever-richening earth, there are giant tracts of monoculture: corn, wheat, soybeans. Three tons of soil—soil it took millennia and geologic events on a grand scale to build—is now squandered for every ton of food produced.

Wisconsin, the first state to ban DDT, is a good starting point for our education about American grasslands, and specifically prairies, because in Wisconsin "new" garden ideas such as replacing your lawn with wildflowers or going native are anything but new. This is largely because of the trickle-down effects of the work at the University of Wisconsin–Madison, where the sixty-acre Curtis Prairie, adjacent to the ancient relict area and long used as cropland and pasture, was brought back to its original state starting in the late 1930s by workers from the Civilian Conservation Corps. The United States has other restorations, both at Madison and elsewhere, but Curtis is the world's oldest, and largest, restored tallgrass prairie, for more than half a century a working laboratory of the prairie's ecology and its plants.

No wonder, then, that people in those parts seem to know their wildflowers, or that in suburban Wisconsin neighborhoods a noticeable number of homeowners have been defying the norm for a decade or two by plowing under their lawns in favor of something wilder. (There are enough such homes in the Milwaukee area alone that an annual prairie-garden tour has been conducted for busloads of interested visitors for more than fifteen years.) Not just local botanists and graduate students found themselves influenced by the prairie restoration movement. Gardeners did, too.

Lorrie Otto started tearing up her lawn north of Milwaukee more than twenty-five years ago. Actually, refraining from mowing was the least of it; Otto went so far as to raze nine eighty-year-old nonnative spruces to let the sun shine in on her would-be

What Diboll calls the "root-to-shoot ratio" is two to one among prairie plants, meaning that two thirds of the plants' biomass is below ground—"a real storehouse," Diboll says—reaching down into the earth to access moisture and meanwhile redistributing nutrients, aerating the soil, and performing other important functions. Even young plants that show only an inch of growth aboveground may already have produced a foot or more of downward life.

Just because prairies never evolve into forests does not mean that they are either static or homogeneous. Prairies, and even small prairie gardens, are ever-changing organisms—plants that dominate this season may recede into the background next year, so wise prairie gardeners never become too attached to a picture-perfect image.

"We must learn to appreciate the innate wisdom of nature's chaos," says Diboll.

Besides grasses, prairies are typically made up of a large number of composites (daisy- or sunflowerlike flowers in the *Compositae* family) and also a high percentage of legumes, such as purple prairie clover (*Petalostemum purpureum*), milk vetch (*Astragalus agrestis*), and leadplant (*Amorpha canescens,* one of the few woody prairie plants). By fixing nitrogen into the soil, the legumes help boost productivity of the grasses; conversely, the grasses also seem to have a beneficial effect on the legumes, which produce more seed when grown in tandem than when grown alone.

Composites across the country. OPPOSITE, FROM LEFT TO RIGHT, TOP ROW TO BOTTOM ROW: *Black-eyed Susan* (Rudbeckia hirta); *boltonia* (Boltonia asteroides); *cup plant* (Silphium perfoliatum); *sneezeweed* (Helenium autumnale); *hardy ageratum, or mist flower* (Eupatorium coelestinum); *garden coreopsis* (Coreopsis tinctoria); *calico aster* (Aster lateriflorus); *Maximilian daisy* (Helianthus maximiliani); *and* Rudbeckia 'Goldsturm', *the famous European cultivar of our native* R. fulgida. RIGHT: *Prairie blazing star* (Liatris pycnostachya).

worth it, Diboll says. To use herbicides, start by mowing in early spring, then spray in midspring, midsummer, and early fall.

To remove unwanted vegetation without chemicals, cultivate every two weeks from early spring through fall, to a depth of four to five inches. Wait no longer than two weeks between cultivation sessions or the plants will begin to reestablish.

In each case, prepare the soil so it is smooth and free of clods, then wait until spring to plant—and only after a final weed-killing treatment is performed. With herbicides, apply when spring weeds are two to three inches high, then cultivate shallowly (just an inch) and plant right away. Only cultivation can be used at this time, too, to a depth of an inch timed a week after the first spring rain occurs, Diboll recommends. Again, plant immediately after treatment.

Lorrie Otto agrees that all existing undesirables must be eliminated.

"You simply must get every last perennial weed out before starting planting," she says, drawing on more than twenty-five years of hands-on experience.

Sometimes, particularly when working with small areas, undesirables can be simply dug out—as when you lift and discard (to the compost pile, please) a section of turfgrass before preparing any garden. Soil solarization—covering the area to be planted with black plastic for most or all of a growing season so that the undesirable plants are cooked and suffocated —is an easy method in small areas, and can even be translated to a large-scale landscape.

Certain soil-building styles may smother existing weeds, too. When Otto wanted to grow prairie plants adapted to sandy soils on her clayey site, she first laid a thick layer of newspaper over the ground, then piled on a very thick layer of leaves, then "great piles of sand," and then repeated the leaves and sand,

"to simulate a sand prairie." Many existing weeds would necessarily be thwarted this way, though it would be impractical for a large-scale planting.

On the topic of soil-improvement, be realistic. Although landscapers typically force grass to grow on a mere three inches of topsoil, deep-rooted prairie plants need much more. While they don't require a double-dug bed full of peat moss and rotted manure (in fact, it is best to avoid manure since it may contain a great number of weed seeds), examine the conditions the plants want in nature and try to approximate them. Two examples: Sand, rotted leaves, and compost can help break up clayey soils, for instance, and organic materials such as the leaves and compost also improve overall soil life that is dangerously low in very acid soils. Follow the instructions provided by your supplier of seeds or plants for best results.

PICKING THE PLANTS

Any prairie garden is necessarily going to be interpretive, since it is man's hand, not nature's, that is doing the designing and planting. To grow a loosely designed meadow is perhaps the easiest way to start using prairie plants. At the New York Botanical Garden, former Native Plants Garden curator Kathryn Venezia advocates minimeadows as lawn alternatives.

"Even a loosely interpreted meadow offers much more botanical diversity than a grass lawn," she says, recommending that gardeners "start small, one hundred square feet at a time" unless helpers and a tractor are at the ready.

Venezia's meadow-making methods: If your lawn is spotty and sparse, you're in luck. You can plug in groups of wildflower transplants without removing the turf first. Simply cultivate patches of the lawn and introduce prairie plants into these prepared spots.

To establish a "new" suburban prairie of her own,
ABOVE, Lorrie Otto placed thick layers of newspaper
over the ground to smother the grass. Next came heaps of
leaves, great piles of sand, more leaves, and more sand to
simulate the sand-prairie soil. This process naturally
thwarted weeds that might have taken over, and it built
the soil. RIGHT: In an older section of Otto's garden, a
romantic vine-covered arch is reminiscent of the days
before she implemented her once-controversial philosophy.

A Palette of Prairie Plants

Though generally rugged, adaptable creatures, prairie grasses and forbs, like any other plants, do have their favorite conditions. The three lists that follow were prepared by Neil Diboll, a prairie ecologist and owner of Prairie Nursery in Wisconsin, whose work can be seen on pages 54–57.

For Dry, Sandy Soils

Amorpha canescens, leadplant
Anemone cylindrica, thimbleweed
Anemone patens, pasqueflower
Asclepias tuberosa, butterfly weed
Aster azureus, sky blue aster
Aster ericoides, heath aster
Aster laevis, smooth aster
Aster ptarmicoides, white aster
Aster sericeus, silky aster
Astragalus canadensis, Canada milk vetch
Callirhoe triangulata, poppy mallow
Campanula rotundifolia, harebell
Coreopsis palmata, stiff coreopsis
Echinacea pallida, pale purple coneflower
Epilobium angustifolium, fireweed
Euphorbia corollata, flowering spurge
Geum triflorum, prairie smoke
Helianthus laetiflorus, showy sunflower
Helianthus mollis, downy sunflower
Helianthus occidentalis, western sunflower
Helianthus strumosus, woodland sunflower
Heuchera richardsonii, alum root
Lespedeza capitata, roundheaded bush clover
Liatris aspera, rough blazing star
Liatris cylindracea, dwarf blazing star
Lithospermum caroliniense, hairy puccoon
Lupinus perennis, lupine
Monarda fistulosa, bergamot
Monarda punctata, dotted mint
Penstemon gracilis, slender beardtongue
Penstemon grandiflorus, beardtongue
Petalostemum purpureum, purple prairie clover
Ranunculus rhomboideus, prairie buttercup
Ratibida pinnata, yellow coneflower
Rudbeckia hirta, black-eyed Susan
Solidago nemoralis, gray goldenrod
Solidago rigida, stiff goldenrod
Solidago speciosa, showy goldenrod
Tradescantia ohiensis, spiderwort
Verbena stricta, hoary vervain

GRASSES
Andropogon gerardii, big bluestem
Andropogon scoparius [*Schizachyrium scoparium*], little bluestem
Bouteloua curtipendula, sideoats grama
Elymus canadensis, Canada wild rye
Koeleria cristata, Junegrass
Panicum virgatum, switchgrass
Sorghastrum nutans, Indian grass
Sporobolus heterolepis, prairie dropseed

For Medium Soils

Allium cernuum, nodding pink onion
Amorpha canescens, leadplant
Anemone cylindrica, thimbleweed
Asclepias syriaca, common milkweed
Asclepias tuberosa, butterfly weed
Aster spp.
Astragalus canadensis, Canada milk vetch
Baptisia leucantha, white false indigo
Baptisia leucophaea, cream false indigo
Cassia hebecarpa, wild senna
Ceanothus americanus, New Jersey tea

CLOCKWISE FROM TOP LEFT: *Big bluestem* (Andropogon gerardii) *dominates the tallgrass prairie; butterfly weed* (Asclepias tuberosa); *Culver's root* (Veronicastrum virginicum); *rattlesnake master* (Eryngium yuccifolium); *New England aster* (Aster novae-angliae).

Coreopsis palmata, stiff
  coreopsis
Desmodium canadense, Canada
  tick trefoil
Dodecatheon meadia, shooting
  star
Echinacea spp., purple
  coneflower
Eryngium yuccifolium,
  rattlesnake master
Euphorbia corollata, flowering
  spurge
Helianthus laetiflorus, showy
  sunflower
Helianthus occidentalis,
  western sunflower
Helianthus strumosus,
  woodland sunflower
Heliopsis helianthoides, oxeye
  sunflower
Heuchera richardsonii, alum
  root
Lespedeza capitata,
  roundheaded bush clover
Liatris aspera, rough blazing
  star
Monarda fistulosa, bergamot
Parthenium integrifolium, wild
  quinine
Penstemon digitalis, smooth
  penstemon
Petalostemum candidum, white
  prairie clover

Petalostemum purpureum,
  purple prairie clover
Ratibida pinnata, yellow
  coneflower
Rudbeckia hirta, black-eyed
  Susan
Rudbeckia subtomentosa, sweet
  black-eyed Susan
Silphium integrifolium,
  rosinweed
Silphium laciniatum, compass
  plant
Silphium terebinthinaceum,
  prairie dock
Solidago rigida, stiff
  goldenrod
Solidago speciosa, showy
  goldenrod
Tradescantia ohiensis,
  spiderwort
Veronicastrum virginicum,
  Culver's root
Zizia aptera, heartleaf golden
  Alexanders

GRASSES
Andropogon gerardii, big bluestem
Elymus canadensis, Canada
  wild rye
Panicum virgatum,
  switchgrass
Sorghastrum nutans, Indian grass
Sporobolus heterolepis, prairie
  dropseed

For Wet Soils

Anemone canadensis, Canada
  anemone
Asclepias incarnata, red
  milkweed
Aster novae-angliae, New
  England aster
Baptisia leucantha, white false
  indigo
Chelone glabra, turtlehead
Coreopsis tripteris, tall
  coreopsis
Desmodium canadense, Canada
  tick trefoil
Dodecatheon meadia, shooting
  star
Eupatorium maculatum, Joe-
  pye weed
Eupatorium perfoliatum,
  boneset
Filipendula rubra, queen-of-
  the-prairie
Gentiana andrewsii, bottle
  gentian
Heuchera richardsonii, alum
  root
Iris shrevei, wild iris
Liatris pycnostachya, prairie
  blazing star
Lilium superbum, Turk's-cap
  lily

Lobelia cardinalis, cardinal
  flower
Lobelia siphilitica, great blue
  lobelia
Monarda fistulosa, bergamot
Ratibida pinnata, yellow
  coneflower
Rudbeckia subtomentosa, sweet
  black-eyed Susan
Silphium integrifolium,
  rosinweed
Silphium perfoliatum, cup
  plant
Silphium terebinthinaceum,
  prairie dock
Solidago rigida, stiff
  goldenrod
Vernonia fasciculata, ironweed
Veronicastrum virginicum,
  Culver's root

GRASSES
Andropogon gerardii, big
  bluestem
Calamagrostis canadensis,
  bluejoint grass
Elymus canadensis, Canada
  wild rye
Spartina pectinata, prairie
  cordgrass

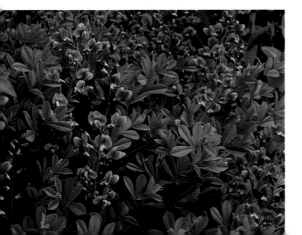

CLOCKWISE FROM TOP
LEFT: Planting for medium
  soil includes pink nodding
  onion (Allium cernuum);
  detail; moist-soil plants such
  as white boneset (Eupatorium
  perfoliatum); cup plant
  (Silphium perfoliatum); blue
  false indigo (Baptisia
  australis).

If the lawn is thick and healthy, the turf is probably best lifted before replanting. Either way, selective hand-weeding is a critical part of follow-up maintenance, and an annual mowing in spring, followed by thorough raking up (and composting) of debris.

Know your aesthetic goal before you order a single plant or seed. If a month-long show is all you want, classic prairie plants and grasses will oblige with their main event from July into August (the grasses then look good as they mellow come fall, and even all winter long once your eye is adjusted to their subtle beauty). An added spring show can be achieved by including in your design a few low-growing "ephemerals," early-season flowers that bloom and fade quickly to make space for main-season plants. Shooting star, downy phlox, and prairie smoke, all springtime bloomers, will happily share the same turf as asters, goldenrods, and sunflowers, for instance.

Whatever your goal, from loose meadow to more traditional grass-dominated prairie, be sure to select a plant list from among those best adapted to your existing (or intended) soil type. A chart of plants for various soil types appears on pages 46–47. Plants well-matched to the site conditions will always win out over those that don't belong, so don't waste money or time on the latter.

SEED OR TRANSPLANTS?

Which raw material—seeds or transplants—would be best for your purposes? Each has its merits, not the least of which is price. At an average of one plant per square foot, a mere one-acre prairie (meaning 43,560 plants, since there are that many square feet per acre) would cost a literal fortune, plus labor, which is roughly figured at twice the plant materials cost. High-quality seed for the same area would cost between approximately four hundred dollars (grasses only) and fifteen hundred dollars (grasses and forbs), not including sowing, which would bring the total to about two thousand dollars an acre. (Remember, neither total includes soil preparation.)

Even the two-thousand-dollar seed-method price may sound high, but think of it this way: If the area under consideration is now in lawn, and you pay even fifty dollars to mow it once a week, by the end of a six-month growing season you have spent more than twelve hundred dollars just for mowing.

Another plus: A seed-grown prairie planting will have more genetic diversity than if you begin with young plants—it will be more like a natural community.

"With transplants, you're growing a garden, not a plant community," says Diboll, his ecologist's orientation surfacing. The reason, he explains, is basically this: It is extremely difficult to replicate the relationships between plants—to site your 43,560 baby plants in a way that they would assemble themselves. And one plant per square foot is a mere fraction of the forty to sixty seeds Diboll typically sows per foot, expecting ten to germinate and four to six to survive. With a seeded planting, you simply start with more individual plants, perhaps six times as many. More plants, more genetic information—more diversity.

Transplants, however, are frequently more reliable —in an unfavorable weather year, certain seeds may never germinate in a nonirrigated seeded planting at all, whereas transplants may have a better chance. Transplants also get off to a faster start since they are already at least a year old, sometimes two, when you buy them. By their second, and certainly third, year in your ground, they will be quite showy and full. Seeded plantings take more like five years to fill in

Prairies started from seed are often sown with "nurse crops," TOP, *such as annual rye, annual flax, or oats to suppress weed growth as desirables become established.*
ABOVE: *Once bison were an integral part of the prairie's success, along with fire and management by native American people. Occasional grazing encourages sturdy plant growth.*

GRASSLAND TIPS

Sun is a must. Don't try to grow prairie plants in the shade.

Don't fertilize. More often than not, fertilizer will just encourage unwanted weeds that lurk in the soil or that blow in from elsewhere.

Match the plants to the site carefully (see the list of plants for various soil types on pages 46–47). If your site is dry, stick to shorter species like little bluestem, sideoats grama, needlegrass, or Junegrass. Giants like big bluestem and Indian grass demand more soil moisture.

Be prepared to wait, especially when starting from seed. Many prairie plants spend their first couple of years developing roots, not flowers.

If you're thinking of introducing transplants into an existing sod, a caveat: It's one thing for baby plants to successfully compete if set into patches carved out among clump-forming bunchgrasses, another for them to make a stand against rhizomatous invaders—plants like lawn grasses that make a nearly impenetrable network of horizontal, modified stems just below the soil surface. Carefully evaluate their opponents.

REKINDLING THE ELEMENT OF FIRE

Fire creates plant diversity, a fact that Native Americans knew well. Many plant communities, from prairie to the scrubby semiarid chaparrals—even Yellowstone, as we learned recently—actually depend on the presence of periodic fires, sometimes spaced years apart, to keep them healthy.

Burning has also long been recognized by farmers as an effective tool for management of fields. Today it may not be possible in some areas to get permission to burn at all. This could be a good chance to teach children about the power, danger, and necessity of fire. Obviously, their safety, and that of pets and property must be considered above all, but we've never heard of a case where a responsible burning went awry. Never start any kind of fire, however small, without checking to see if it is both safe and legal to do so in your area. In agricultural zones, gaining approval may be as simple as calling the fire tower to alert them; in more populated zones, you may have to apply for a permit and have the fire department on hand. Contact your local agricultural extension service or botanic garden for more detailed instructions. Never use any gasoline, chemical agents, or discarded tires (an

old and very hazardous farm trick) to start a fire.

The timing of a burn depends on the desired annihilation or encouragement—what are you trying to set back, and what are you trying to promote? To reduce cool-season weed grasses like bluegrass in a meadow or prairie planting, but stimulate warm-season prairie grass species, burning must be timed after the former starts growing but before the latter has put on much growth—mid- to late spring. Burning then will also set back cool-season weeds, sedges, and forbs, which may not figure into your plan.

Sometimes dormant-season (late winter or early spring) burns are better. This can only be determined by knowing the growing habits of *all* the plants in the target area.

Even if your management strategy dictates a particular time for burning, it simply may not be possible. Is there enough fuel (old dried plant material) to get a fire going? If not, wait another growing season for more fuel to build up, or mow instead.

Even the lightest rain can moisten the "fuel" sufficiently to make burning impossible. Windy days are not meant for burning.

Always burn in sections,

like a crazy quilt. Map out the sections with your mower, and mow double-wide paths between them with the blade on its lowest setting. Then moisten these firebreaks with water.

Consider burning only part of the entire planting in a single year; burning the whole thing may eliminate overwintering butterfly chrysalises and other beneficial insects, as well as bird nesting sites.

The black ash returns nutrients to the soil and absorbs heat from the sun, warming the soil faster. It will disappear soon beneath emerging plants.

In some cases, burning actually helps the opponent. Fire scarifies the seed of white sweet clover (*Melilotus alba*), for example, perhaps the number-one enemy of prairie makers (even in Brooklyn, New York). Country Wetlands Nursery recommends pulling it at the time of petal drop instead.

Don't underestimate the heat or rapid movement of even a small fire. A hose and a strong water supply are essential, as are enough people armed with metal rakes and shovels to manage each section. Start with a tiny section—ten by ten feet—to see how fire works.

If you're nervous about fire, don't try this method.

(this estimate is based on a diverse seed mix of grasses and other perennials, not one loaded with showy, flash-in-the-pan annuals).

It sounds like a mix of seeds and transplants would be the best of all, but it's not. A mix causes a management nightmare, since the seeded area must be mowed regularly the first couple of years (to about six inches) to retard weeds, and transplants would recover slowly if mown down.

An area of transplants could be used, however, to disguise a slower-growing seeded area—say a wide swath of plants at the most visible edge of your seeded planting, so that it will appear at least from a distance that things are really off to a quick start.

Seeding is often done in late spring or early summer to take advantage of warm weather, which prairie plants favor. Remember: You will be doing a final early spring preparation of the seedbed to eliminate more of the undesirable cool-season weeds, so early planting is neither possible nor useful. However, many forb seeds require a period of cool stratification —cold and moisture—to break dormancy, meaning that they may lie dormant until that need is satisfied. Some nurseries dry-stratify the seeds (put them in a refrigerator to simulate the winter that many seeds need to undergo in order to germinate) in advance of selling them to you and you need only moisten and refrigerate them for several weeks before sowing. There are other more specialized cases, too; ask your seed supplier for specific instructions.

Fire is an important tool for prairie makers, OPPOSITE, LEFT. *They burn in small sections, delineated by mowed strips,* OPPOSITE, RIGHT, *that are water-soaked for firebreaks. These edges can be made amazingly precise. The Sauk prairie restoration in Wisconsin,* LEFT, *might be a candidate for late spring burning. The burn kills the early-emerging alien weeds. The dark color of the burned ash absorbs sunlight and warms the ground, giving the late-to-sprout natives a head start while contributing nutritious ash to the plants.*

ORNAMENTAL AMERICAN GRASSES

Ornamental grasses have won favor in recent years as naturalistic additions to the landscape, but many current favorites—*Miscanthus* and *Pennisetum,* for instance—are actually invasive foreigners. They have demonstrated an inclination to self-sow around the landscape, while simultaneously doubling in girth each season. A very watchful eye must be kept on such aliens as the Mediterranean and Australian grasses being promoted in horticulture today—they are fine for the conscientious collector but perhaps not for less-attentive gardeners.

Fortunately, grasses needn't be exotic to be ornamental; many American species are at least as handsome. Improved forms are being selected out of native populations by a number of nurseries. Here are some to consider:

BIG BLUESTEM (*Andropogon gerardii*) was the primary grass of the original tallgrass prairie that ranged from Ohio to Colorado. Usually five or six feet tall, it can approach eight or even ten feet in a perfect site, where there is ample soil moisture in the warm-weather months. It has blue summertime foliage and bronze fall color. Selections have been made for southern climates, sandy soil, improved fall color, and other traits. Look for related species.

LITTLE BLUESTEM (*Schizachyrium scoparium* or *Andropogon scoparius*) is a shortgrass species usually reaching about three feet. Like its taller counterpart, little blue is a warm-season clump-former. Besides hillsides and prairies, it also inhabits open woodland areas that receive good light. Fall color can range from bronze to purple-red. Selections are being made for true blue foliage and other qualities.

INDIAN GRASS (*Sorghastrum nutans*) is another native of the tallgrass prairie, though it usually reaches only three feet. The foliage of this beautiful grass can be green, grayish green, or blue—the last being one of the favored characteristics, and a form called 'Sioux Blue' has been named to celebrate its beauty.

PRAIRIE CORDGRASS (*Spartina pectinata*) is a denizen of low-lying areas where moisture is ample, as at the water's edge. This spreading grass has graceful arching leaves that take on yellow fall color. A gold-margined variety called 'Aureomarginata' is even more ornamental.

PRAIRIE DROPSEED (*Sporobolus heterolepis*) forms two-foot hummocks of arching emerald green leaves, which are topped in August with flowerheads that have a distinct fragrance that faintly recalls buttered popcorn.

CLOCKWISE FROM TOP LEFT: *Indian grass* (Sorghastrum nutans); *and flower detail; northern (or inland) sea oats* (Chasmanthium latifolium); *little bluestem* (Schizachyrium scoparium *or* Andropogon scoparius); *golden grass* (Milium effusum *'Aureum'*); *switchgrass* (Panicum virgatum).

SWITCHGRASS (*Panicum virgatum*) is versatile and much appreciated by wildlife as winter and early spring cover. Its fall color is exceptional, usually yellow. It is typically three or four feet tall. The selection 'Heavy Metal' has steel-blue summer foliage and turns bright yellow in fall; 'Hanse Herms' is orange-red to burgundy in fall.

DEERGRASS (*Muhlenbergia rigens*) is a standout for dry western gardens, where it can retain its green color despite low summertime moisture. Its foliage is about three feet tall, with long-lasting whiplike flowers borne above it in summer. It is excellent for holding coastal slopes. Other "muhlies" being promoted for landscaping include *M. lindheimeri* (Lindheimer muhly), with its clumps of blue foliage, and *M. filipes* (purple muhly), a southeastern native with purple flowerheads.

CALIFORNIA FESCUE (*Festuca californica*) is a clumping, medium-height California native for dry areas in sun or part shade, reaching about two to three feet tall. Selections with good blue color are particularly desirable, and turn purplish at frost. The selection 'Salmon Creek' is blue-gray flushed with burgundy.

RIBBON GRASS (*Phalaris arundinacea* 'Picta'), also called gardener's garters, is a showy grass variegated green and white, that is tol-erant of part shade. It is highly ornamental, but also zealous, so keep a careful eye on its movements. Avoid the species, which is troublesome in wetlands. Good for holding banks in moist soil, which it favors.

SIDEOATS GRASS (*Bouteloua curtipendula*) is medium sized, with highly ornamental flowerheads touched with orange and purple followed by decorative oatlike seeds. Grow it in dry to medium soil.

NORTHERN SEA OATS (*Chasmanthium latifolium*) turns from green to copper in fall and then to a wheat brown. Its seedheads are among the most beautiful of any grass, drooping and shaped like tiny flattened pinecones. Northern sea oats prefers rich, moist soil and part shade, but is adaptable to other conditions.

BUFFALO GRASS (*Buchloe dactyloides*) is an outstanding native lawn substitute, using little fertilizer and water. Research at Texas A&M (which released the all-female variety 'Prairie') and the University of Nebraska (the variety '609', also female) is continuing to breed better buffalo grass—shorter, darker color and one requiring even less mowing. A native of the middle third of the country, it is now being tested as far east as New Jersey, where the wetter climate is not exactly the twelve to twenty-four inches of water per year that buffalo grass likes—yet.

RIGHT, TOP TO BOTTOM: *Meadow muhly* (Muhlenbergia rigens, *detail in winter*); *a specimen of meadow muhly; split beard bluestem* (Andropogon ternarius, *detail in winter*). *Many of the grasses become most ornamental after the autumn frost.*

NEIL DIBOLL
WESTFIELD, WISCONSIN

THERE IS THE SMELL OF BUT-
tered popcorn in the air, or is it
fresh cilantro? Neither, Neil Diboll, owner of the Prairie Nursery, assures his perplexed guests
—it's August, when the aroma
of ripening prairie dropseed
(*Sporobolus heterolepis*), one of the
most beautiful of native prairie
grasses, wafts through the fields.

Diboll's attention is quickly
turned to one clump of the dropseed among thousands growing
in orderly rows at Prairie Nursery in Westfield, Wisconsin,

PRINCE OF THE PRAIRIE

which he has owned for more
than a decade.

"I used to be an ecologist, but
they're turning me into a horti-
culturist," says Diboll, spying a
plant with distinctive yellow
stems unlike the rest of the crop.
He'll transplant the "better" one
to a special observation bed to
see if it merits a future as a named
selection.

The yellow-stemmed prairie
dropseed, or one of many glau-
cous selections of little bluestem
that he is propagating to name—
all of these are examples of phe-
notypic variation, natural occur-
rences within a larger population
that display measurably distinctive traits. The difference may be
purely aesthetic, like the yel-
lower or bluer stems of certain
clumps of a grass species, or
qualities like greater resistance to
disease, a longer bloom period, a
dwarfer form, and so on.

The future of native plants,
horticulturists agree, is in making selections that are just a little
better for garden use than the

*A monoculture is never encouraged
in an intentional planting except
in a nursery where harvesting specific
plants or pure seeds necessitates this*

*isolation. At Prairie Nursery,
plantings such as these of* Liatris
and Veronicastrum, RIGHT, *are
attractive to visitors, including a
monarch butterfly that lands on a
nearby purple coneflower,* ABOVE.

general population—and the scientist in Diboll concurs, if a bit grudgingly.

Diboll doesn't fancy himself a designer; most of his projects are large-scale restorations. He does, however, have some observations on design. There are basically three prevailing approaches to prairie planting, he notes: the general method ("plant 'em all and let God sort it out!"); the patchwork prairie (plant many different "subcommunities"); and the "artsy" prairie (plant drifts and masses in specific areas).

The first, usually accomplished by seeding, is likely to yield the most diverse and functional prairie, since what grows from among the many species you sow will be those best adapted to the site and other existing conditions. The patchwork method allows for the creation of several different kinds of prairies in the space: a shortgrass mix in one area, for instance, with a tallgrass area nearby—distinct habitats that appeal to different wildlife. (A tip: Keep the shortgrass to the north and west of the tall, which will otherwise seed into and overrun the little ones.)

In the artsy prairie, monotypic waves of a single plant can even be planted for drama—which,

Diboll says, will certainly catch the eye, but its value shouldn't be overrated. "When only one, or maybe two or three species of flowers are planted in an area, one doth not a community create," he warns.

At the nursery, of course, that very approach has to be taken to propagate efficiently, and whole blocks of a single species in bloom, though hardly recommended, are indeed arresting. Tasty, too, it seems. A goldfinch perches on a barely ripe seedhead of prairie blazing star (*Liatris pynostachya*), capturing Diboll's attention—and stealing a bit of next year's inventory. No matter. "It's a total bird restaurant," he says of the nursery fields in his characteristically positive style.

Despite the negative facts and figures on shrinking biodiversity that he knows all too well as a scientist, Diboll's is an upbeat, and infectious, message: that through restoring native-plant communities, we can make a difference.

"We're like adolescents becoming adults," he says of the United States. "Our mandate was to subdue the environment. . . . Now we realize that people are becoming extraneous to the environment and we have to learn to live *with* it."

TOP: *Rocky Mountain blazing star* (Liatris ligulistylis).
CENTER: *Queen-of-the-prairie* (Filipendula rubra).
LEFT: *Cardinal flower* (Lobelia cardinalis).
OPPOSITE, ABOVE: *One species, oxeye sunflower* (Heliopsis helianthoides), *is grown on its own, not just to be pretty but to facilitate the harvest of pure seed.*
BELOW: *Prairie dropseed* (Sporobolus heterolepis) *in the nursery rows.*

DICK AND MARSHA
KRUEGER
MEQUON, WISCONSIN

MORE THAN A DECADE HAS passed since Dick and Marsha Krueger's Kentucky bluegrass lawn gave way to something more accurately Wisconsin: a miniature prairie, backed by a shrubby edge composed principally of highbush blueberries (*Vaccinium corymbosum*).

Both front and backyard were begun simultaneously, but using different methods. Because of serious drainage problems and construction relating to an easement, the front of the property required extensive regrading, so

A LAWN LONG GONE

BELOW: *Flowers for indoors.*
ABOVE TOP RIGHT: *When extensive regrading of the front yard was complete, the Kruegers opted for a natural alternative to lawn.* ABOVE RIGHT: *Mowing*

was stopped in parts of the backyard, and young plants were plugged in to dominate the bluegrass. OPPOSITE, ABOVE: *The front yard in August.* BELOW: *Lawn makes a dramatic contrast to the prairie.*

it was scraped to bare clay, then seeded with a mixture of native grasses and forbs including baptisia, silphiums, bee balm, and coneflowers.

Behind the house, the Kruegers simply stopped mowing the bluegrass and plugged in transplants of desirable prairie species, which over time have come to dominate the former lawn-grass monoculture. Between the front and back miniprairies, a portion of the place is still closely mown, providing a stark contrast to the shaggy native portions and also serving as a reminder—a shrinking reminder, since every year the remaining lawn gives way to a few more wildflowers—of how dull and lifeless the yard used to be.

Today, each area continues to develop and evolve mainly by the emergence of self-sown seedlings—those left behind by the birds, that is—but the Kruegers regularly add a few plants, too,

and Dick gives the prairie a little help by collecting the seeds himself and scratching them in.

He does an annual mowing in spring, followed by a thorough raking to simulate the effects of burning. Regular hand-weeding reduces pesky invaders like Queen Anne's lace, ragweed, white sweet clover, and curly dock—remnants of the old field that covered the whole street before the houses were built, whose seeds still lurk in the soil. Krueger describes his maintenance routine as a simple one, and it is clearly one performed with love.

"He is the custodial parent," says Marsha, who brings the prairie inside with bouquets of fresh flowers. "I was just a birthmother."

CHICAGO BOTANIC
GARDEN
GLENCOE, ILLINOIS

NO ONE EVER TOLD CURA-
tor Kristin Perry that powdery
mildew, rodents, and sunflowers
would prove her most stubborn
opponents in the job as curator of the Chicago Botanic Garden's quarter-acre demonstration
prairie garden. To expect the unexpected is the byword of habitat-
style gardening, and since she
took the job in 1985, Perry has
learned as much as she can from

A NEW PRAIRIE PRIMER

*The quarter-acre demonstration
prairie garden at the Chicago
Botanic Garden exhibits a planting
scheme for local home owners.
This controlled space utilizes*

*mown grass paths to make the
plantings accessible,* RIGHT, *and
brick mowing strips make their
maintenance easy—no edging
is necessary, the mower wheels
just drive along the brick border.
Plants such as red milkweed
(Asclepias incarnata),* ABOVE,
*can be viewed as visitors walk
along the paths.*

the surprises of the trail-blazing
garden.

A strip of brick delineates
mown from unmown areas in
the demo garden, and stockade
fencing further lends a sense of
home, as if someone has turned a
backyard into a miniprairie.
Though charming, the fence has
proved somewhat of a hin-
drance, since it restricts air circulation and thereby encourages
powdery mildew, particularly on
the grasses. Little and big bluestem and prairie dropseed are
troubled by the mildew, says
Perry; panic grass (*Panicum virgatum*) doesn't seem to succumb.

Besides the grasses, bergamot
(*Monarda fistulosa*), rattlesnake
master (*Eryngium yuccifolium*),
purple coneflower (*Echinacea purpurea*), Culver's root (*Veronicastrum virginicum*), nodding onion
(*Allium cernuum*), obedient plant
(*Physostegia virginiana*), butterfly
weed (*Asclepias tuberosa*), compass plant and prairie dock (*Silphium* spp.), red milkweed
(*Asclepias incarnata*), and senna
(*Cassia hebecarpa*) comingle in the
planting. Woody members of the

THERE IS A TIME AND A place to garden, and a time and a place simply to let things be. Discerning one from the other is the lesson in the rolling fields at Tower Hill Botanic Garden in Boylston, Massachusetts, where the community of grasses and forbs is particularly handsome from midsummer through fall.

But how to accomplish such understated beauty, particularly on a large and unevenly graded site such as this? By doing very little at all—far less, even, than

FIELDS OF DREAMS

The field at Tower Hill Botanic Garden, RIGHT, *is a managed grassland. Mowing takes the place of burning or grazing for the*

purpose of maintaining the dominance of the grasses and forbs. Without mowing, the field would become woodland. ABOVE: *Swallows and bluebirds are attracted to the boxes dotted throughout the fields.*

if the same area were managed as lawn, and with lower cost and more rewarding results.

"A field is supposed to be simple and pleasurable, not complicated," says John Trexler, director of Tower Hill, and his prescribed regimen bears out that philosophy.

A single mowing, timed after the first killing frost (late October or early November, in a typical year) is the mainstay of the field-management program at Tower Hill, headquarters of the Worcester County Horticultural Society, one of the nation's oldest horticultural organizations. The fallen material is left right where the tractor blades put it, and from it many seeds will serve as food for wildlife, or sprout over time, with the remaining debris gradually returning to the soil—all that isn't carried off by birds the next spring for nesting material, that is.

A system of paths is mown into the fields; again, says Trexler, keep it simple.

"Paths come about because you want to get from Point A to Point B. Follow the contours of the land and make the route as comfortable as you can—truly the path of least resistance." (If you have a dog, watch where it walks. It will define a path for you.)

Because there are almost no "problem" plants in the natural makeup of this field dominated by little bluestem (*Schizachyrium scoparium*), other maintenance chores are minimal. Poison ivy (*Toxicodendron radicans*) did move in, seeded around by birds when the fields were in pre–botanic-garden years. Now, after the bobolinks and other grass-nesters have finished their reproductive cycle (about August), gardeners attack patches by spot spraying with herbicide. (Poison ivy can also be cut down and dug out. Never burn the remains; the smoke is toxic.)

"Fields make ideal antechambers between one studied garden area and another," says Trexler, "a calming, uncomplicated habitat."

ABOVE: *Paths are mowed through the field to keep them open for visitors all summer.* RIGHT: *In fall, fading grasses and goldenrod enhance the foliage colors of the trees.*

THE TRIANGLE GARDEN
BROOKLYN, NEW YORK

NOW, HERE'S A STORY ABOUT those worst-case scenarios I referred to earlier. Even without a bucketful of the original topsoil or one living native plant within a twenty-mile radius, there is hope. I am especially familiar with disastrous sites, having gardened on a rooftop in Manhattan's SoHo district, and more recently in ground-level urban sites in Brooklyn.

On my old roof, many prairie plants proved especially well-suited to exposure to baking sun, wind, and the drought-simulat-

THE WORST OF TIMES

ing conditions of life in containers. The knowledge I gained there was helpful recently, when I was asked to develop a design for a triangular (one-hundred-by-eighty-by-sixty-foot) rubble-filled vacant lot near my city home that people wanted to turn into a park. Some local factions wanted a traditional community garden with vegetable plots, others a formal park, and so on, but when we discovered that the budget for the whole project was a hundred dollars, we agreed seeds were all we could afford. After trucking in clean fill of practically pure sand, provided by a local community-garden agency, some peat moss, and rotted leaf compost that we obtained free from a nearby municipal site, I bought a hundred dollars' worth of seeds of prairie-type plants that had thrived on my city rooftop. After all, I reasoned, this place was like a prairie—hot and dry in summer, freezing in winter.

In a highly visible community garden, OPPOSITE, ABOVE, *quick color was a priority, so annuals and biennials were sown the first season. Plants used*

included, LEFT TO RIGHT FROM ABOVE, *the variable form of black-eyed Susan* (Rudbeckia hirta) *'Gloriosa' daisy; California poppy* (Eschscholzia californica); *another 'Gloriosa' daisy; and garden coreopsis* (Coreopsis tinctoria).

The blend of seeds used wasn't what I would recommend in most cases, since it included such showy annuals as cosmos and sunflowers. However, with the whole community looking on, I figured we'd better have a colorful show the very first year.

The cosmos did prove to be a mistake, since they self-sow prodigiously in the following year, but they have faded for the most part as the garden has given way to American perennials like coreopsis and black-eyed Susan. In the third year, when the perennials took over, the garden was its best ever, and we hardly needed to water. Though our garden isn't a true prairie of grasses and forbs, I can assure you that whatever local wildlife had survived decades of asphalt confinement were happy to see even these familiar, if insufficiently diverse, floral faces.

Meadow-style plantings like the one at the Triangle Garden are probably the most popularized form of native-plant garden to date, and seeds and nursery plants for some of them have been available for a number of years. Growing more complete habitat gardens like most of the ones in this book, made up almost exclusively of locally appropriate native-plant species, has been a challenge until very recently. Today there is no excuse for a "meadow in a can" or a woodland underplanted in Asian astilbe species when reputable native-plant nurseries have become so widespread that there are outstanding vendors to buy from in every region.

P. CLIFFORD MILLER
LAKE FOREST, ILLINOIS

COMPARED TO MANY OF HIS clients' properties, landscape designer P. Clifford Miller's double city lot in Lake Forest, Illinois—a mere 50 wide by 270 feet deep—is confining indeed. But Miller, a proponent of the plant-community–based approach to landscaping, has managed to pack bits of several locally appropriate habitats into his environment nonetheless.

Beyond the house and garage is a patio, and then a bit of lawn —just enough to suit the recreational needs of Miller's small

LEARNING TO LET GO

Despite the confining scale of his small town lot, landscape designer P. Clifford Miller manages to have just enough backyard lawn for his

kids, surrounded by a miniprairie, OPPOSITE, TOP, *in which common milkweed* (Asclepias syriaca, ABOVE) *flourishes. He also has a touch of woods (with cimicifuga and ferns),* OPPOSITE, FAR RIGHT, *and even a small wetland in the form of a tiny pond, planted with blue-flowered pickerelweed* (Pontederia cordata) *and arrow arum* (Peltandra virginica), RIGHT.

children, no more. The turf is surrounded by a swath of mini-prairie, and an electric fence; a group of pines and hemlocks forms a scaled-down north woods. He has a touch of savanna, a little ravine, and even a wetland, in the form of a small pond, with arrow arum (*Peltandra virginica*) and pickerelweed (*Pontederia cordata*)—truly a case of mixed ecological use in a small space.

Miller could develop any one of these miniature systems into a larger theme, he knows, but some plants are taking up too much room. "My problem is that like a lot of plantsmen I haven't let go of some plants," he says. "I have too many rhododendrons. I'm still attached to my Japanese maple and Kousa dogwood. I get more and more toward the natural every year, but I'm not there yet."

One thing that will help, Miller says, is when better forms of more native plants become available in the nursery trade. Although a growing number of nurseries are devoted to enlarging the native repertoire, production of natives still lags far behind that of "standard" landscape fare. "We've put billions into development of roses and carnations," he says, "but hardly a nickel into a *Viburnum lentago* that resists mildew."

2.5 ACRES, PARK VIEW

This landscape's inner area, OPPOSITE, *at the front of the house includes a small lawn and a "collection" area of more traditional perennials such as Sedum 'Autumn Joy', with columbine, prairie dropseed, and other native wildflowers mixed in. In the field beyond,* ABOVE, *part of a park preserve established by the Lake Forest Open Lands group when the neighborhood was formed around it, yellow coneflower dominates the scene in summertime.*

SAFEGUARDING OPEN SPACES and building homes seem two pursuits in opposition, but that did not prove the case when the Lake Forest Open Lands group wanted to make a park on thirty acres of Illinois cornfield.

The creative solution: Instead of developing the whole parcel, the nonprofit organization coordinated the project, selling homesites on just half the land, with the proceeds establishing the rest as West Skokie Nature Preserve.

The owners were attracted by the possibility of building on a site adjacent to land that would remain open, and designer P. Clifford Miller, who also consulted on the park, helped them make their two and a half acres into a three-part landscape.

The property, a former bur oak savanna, had become more "a jungle," Miller recalls, "with lots of invasive aliens." A portion is now modeled after savanna, and another section is an oak woodland.

The fact that such forward-thinking developments continue to be built is encouraging, stirring the hope that more and more people will eventually come to understand the ethic and aesthetic of habitat-style landscaping, where the homeowner is just one small part, instead of master of it all.

Closest to the house is a mix of popular herbaceous nonnatives like *Sedum* 'Autumn Joy'—the collection area. Even within these confines, prairie-region natives are represented. Echoing the parkland are prairie dropseed (*Sporobolus heterolepis*) and columbine (*Aquilegia canadensis*).

"They help carry the feel of the prairie right up to the front door," says Miller.

PRIVATE RESIDENCE
LAKE BLUFF, ILLINOIS

"A GOOD, ESTABLISHED PRAI-
rie requires not much more ex-
pense than a matchstick once a
year," natural landscape designer
P. Clifford Miller is fond of saying, and then proving, to his incredulous clients.

At this private residence in
Lake Bluff, Illinois, that statement proved particularly relevant, since the owners were
thinking of installing lawn on
the thirty-acre cornfield running
down to the shore of Lake Michigan that became their yard.
Or they were, at least, until
Miller made them look at all the

WHAT PRICE, PRAIRIE?

*The owners were going to sow seed
for a lawn on the thirty-acre former
cornfield that became their yard.*

*Instead, they planted a prairie with
flowers such as goldenrod,
ABOVE, which now stretches to
Lake Michigan, TOP RIGHT, to
a lone giant oak, ABOVE
RIGHT, the remaining trace of a
onetime savanna. Wide pathways,
OPPOSITE, TOP, provide access
to the house, OPPOSITE, BOTTOM.*

possibilities and also the costs.

It would have been difficult or
impossible to mow the steep
slope leading down to the lake,
and Miller also knew that the
prairie plants could tolerate the
strong breezes off the water and
that he could count on their deep
roots to hold the soil and prevent
erosion.

"I explained that a prairie
could go in for a lot less than it
would cost to maintain that large
a lawn each year," says Miller,
who designed a meadow mix of
prairie plants instead for the site,
which was subsequently drill-
seeded into the old fields.
Goldenrods (*Solidago* spp.), prairie coneflower (*Ratibida columnifera*), big bluestem (*Andropogon
gerardii*), gaillardia (*Gaillardia*
spp.), and purple coneflowers
(*Echinacea purpurea*) are just a few
of the colorful members of the
meadow.

At one corner of the largest

prairie where they are planted, a
giant single oak tree is now a
monument to the Wisconsin savanna, and a lone bench below it
has become a place to contem-
plate the now-rare habitat.

Today, the owners do not lis-
ten to the weekly sound of mow-
ers, or pay a lawn-maintenance
bill. Nor do they have to buy and
apply fertilizer and herbicides
and other lawn-care supplies.
Their landscape is now a health-
ier environment, not only for
wild visitors but for domestic
pets such as the family dog, too.

The meadow is basically on its
own—all except for a match, to
start the annual springtime burn.

PRIVATE RESIDENCE
AUSTIN, TEXAS

AUSTIN LIES BETWEEN THE two Texases, the richer woodland soils and the drier, hilly parts of the state. This private residence codesigned by Kay Wagenknecht-Harte and Environmental Survey Consulting had to take into account that blend of disparate elements, despite its tiny, half-acre scale. In all, 150 species of plants are represented.

Hints of prairie, savanna, and woodland came into play in what David Mahler of Environmental Survey calls "a combined land-

SUBURBAN SAVANNA

Under a natural canopy of native oaks and cedar elms, TOP RIGHT, *shade-tolerant shrubs, forbs, and grasses were planted,* RIGHT, SECOND FROM TOP. *Bold stonework helped to create*

workable areas from this hilly half-acre lot, BOTTOM RIGHT, *and even made a level for a bench,* ABOVE. *Shrubby cenizo* (Leucophyllum candidum), *with its silvery leaves and purple flowers, likes the sunnier spots,* RIGHT, THIRD FROM TOP. OPPOSITE: *The grass meadow muhly* (Muhlenbergia rigens) *and rich pink salvia* (Salvia greggii) *are featured accent plants.*

scape/habitat restoration." Existing large trees included Texas oak, shin oak, and cedar elm, and they were underplanted with shade-tolerant shrubs and forbs like Turk's-cap mallow (*Malvaviscus arboreus*) and grasses like northern, or inland, sea oats (*Chasmanthium latifolium*), whose seedheads are particularly ornamental.

Other principal grasses used among the more than twenty on the property include big muhly (*Muhlenbergia lindheimeri*), which makes a bold statement as a specimen or en masse, and little bluestem (*Andropogon scoparius* or *Schizachyrium scoparium*). Silvery-foliaged cenizo, a shrubby plant with lavender flowers, is striking against the bold stonework, and more color is created in the sunnier areas with bursts of liatris (*Liatris mucronata*), plateau goldeneye (*Viguiera dentata*), Texas bluebells (*Eustoma grandiflorum*), penstemon (*Penstemon co-*

A PRAIRIE SHOWS ITS AGE—
to those who can read its wrinkles. Owen Conservation Park of the City of Madison, Wisconsin, is a living chronology of the early stages in succession of prairie plantings. Every couple of years since 1980, the park has added five acres to its prairie landscape. The thirty-five or so acres completed thus far form a timeline—from a mass of indistinguishable infant plants, to baby prairie full of medium-height flowers like rudbeckia and echinacea, to adolescents where

LIVES OF A PRAIRIE

taller grasses and forbs have begun to arrive, to nearly adult prairies, with grasses like big bluestem dominating as the forbs wane.

Owen Conservation Park was prairie before the first settlers reached the area, naturalists speculate, but for more than a century, at least, it had been otherwise. The park is named for a former professor at the nearby University of Wisconsin, who in the 1890s bought the land as a summer retreat, raising pigs and other barnyard animals in a farmlike setting. The land was purchased by the City of Madison in 1972, and eight years later, once old fencerows of small trees (principally buckthorn, black locust, and Norway maple) were removed and prairie seeds were sown, the old fields of alien chicory, Queen Anne's lace, and daisies slowly gave way to prairie. Although the area had been grazed, and the smaller understory trees diminished, a nice

The former caretaker's house, BELOW, *is the only trace of the farm that is now Owen Conservation Park. Today the land supports young prairies in various stages of succession. In summer, yellow coneflower* (Ratibida pinnata) *and other sun-colored composites bask in the light,* NEAR RIGHT. *The older plantings,* OPPOSITE, FAR RIGHT, *have become more of a democratic planting of grasses and forbs.*

example of savanna, one of Wisconsin's rarest plant communities, exists on the property, and it is being rekindled.

Today, it is not barnyard animals but birds that inhabit the place, notably bluebirds, sedge wrens, yellowthroats, and, in spring and fall, woodcock and meadowlark. The prairies are managed principally by springtime burning, but seeds are harvested in fall and shared with other conservation parks undertaking the same kind of work. Care is taken to exempt a portion of the prairie from burning each time to protect a share of overwintering butterfly chrysalises.

On almost any summertime day you will see adult butterflies in abundance, and during their migration there is a special treat: hordes of monarchs roosting on the big oaks in the savanna near eveningtime, waiting until morning when the sun will warm them so they can continue on their journey.

A caretaker's house still stands on the site, but Owen's original home is long gone. Traces of him remain, though, in the form of vegetation: A lover of landscaping, he left behind many exotic plants, including a legacy of periwinkle in the surrounding woodlands.

SARA STEIN
POUND RIDGE, NEW YORK

AUTHOR SARA STEIN ISN'T just a gardener, but a naturalist as well. So when it came time to begin landscaping the property that she and her husband, Marty, had bought in the late 1970s, one of her inclinations was just to let the lawn grow.

The results were beautiful. In the first year countless "wild-flowers" bloomed, and the second year was good, too. But then Stein realized that something wasn't working. By the third year, what had looked like dainty flowers—oxeye daisy and

INTERPRETING THE LAND

On a tiny man-made island in her pond, BELOW, *Sara Stein plugged in prairie dropseed* (Sporobolus heterolepis), *making planting holes with a bulb planter, then*

tossing in a little topsoil and a young plant. Elsewhere, Stein is hard at work turning old fields, TOP RIGHT, *into prairie-style plantings,* OPPOSITE. *Crabapples with small fruits to attract birds are planted in a walled garden,* CENTER RIGHT. *Among her many successful birdhouses is a cluster of hollow gourds,* BOTTOM RIGHT.

Queen Anne's lace, for instance —had joined forces with choking thugs such as horse nettle, mug-wort, Canada thistle, and bind-weed to make a full-scale mess. This was no way to create a meadow, she realized; it had be-come a jungle of alien field weeds. Only one native plant was even represented, little bluestem (*Schizachyrium scopar-ium*), a grass that her father called "poverty grass" because it would grow anywhere, even on the poorest soil.

She decided to take the first step toward making a real meadow, the beginning of an ex-periment with native plants that continues today.

Stein started by carefully pre-paring the site, eliminating all ex-isting vegetation, then sowed seeds that required some water-ing at first to become established. Along the shore of a pond at the rear of the property, plugs (young nursery plants) were used

to speed erosion control. Swamp milkweed (*Asclepias incarnata*), Joe-pye weed (*Eupatorium macu-latum*), New York ironweed (*Vernonia noveboracensis*), and sweet black-eyed Susan (*Rud-beckia subtomentosa*) were in-stalled. Then, when the pond was rehabilitated, the last bit of

clay dredged from the bottom was used to make an island.

"This is blue clay," says Stein, "devoid of anything organic. It turns to concrete when it dries." The Steins used a bulb planter on the island and made five hundred holes like clay flowerpots, into which they put prairie dropseed plants and store-bought bagged topsoil. "It worked—all of the prairie dropseed plants took and have grown into the hard clay."

The easiest kind of meadow to make is a monoculture of grass, like prairie dropseed or switchgrass, but that isn't the best kind, says Stein, who works instead with a variety of prairie grasses and forbs. Culver's root (*Veronicastrum virginicum*), rudbeckia, and liatris are just a few showy species she has sown. Since her Pound Ridge, New York, property has more rain and generally moister summers than true prairie country, this is more meadow than prairie, but she chooses those plants that will be as at home here as in Kansas.

To prevent succession to woodland from occurring in her meadows, Stein burns each section every third year (rotating this way spares two thirds of the butterflies and other overwintering desirables). It would take a day to burn the whole thing, she figures, meaning that all the work required to maintain these established sites is a day every three years.

Burning permits from the local health department are required, and Stein prepared her application carefully. Her explanation that she was growing protected plants helped sell the authorities and get her the permit.

The black gold left behind from the burn absorbs sunlight and warms the soil faster, waking the sleeping prairie plants as if by magic.

Sara Stein created a little woodland of native river birch (Betula nigra 'Heritage'), OPPOSITE, TOP ROW; *two European clump birch were delivered by mistake— without spraying, these two languished and died. Butterflies are drawn to asclepias, both the red (Asclepias incarnata),* ABOVE, *and orange (A. tuberosa),* LEFT. *There is much for the birds, too, including nesting boxes,* FAR LEFT.

long one, and unusual. After winter, there is a spring season of wonderful growth, then as the weather heats up to extreme intensity in June, many plants enter a period of semidormancy. Some have produced basal growth, as northern plants might in fall, so when things begin to cool in August, they send up flower spikes. This second wave may not be as showy as in spring, but is nonetheless a boon to gardeners who know how to use it.

A tour of nearby wildflower meadows yielded confirmation of the case for informed management of land. Land that was grazed continually had little or no floral show, save a blossom of thorny Texas bull nettle (*Cnidoscolus texanus*); areas that were fenced off and "protected" in the name of conservation also had little going on, and had moved a step or two along the path of succession to a shrubby tangle. Land that was lightly grazed was the most diverse of all—a strong point in favor of appropriate management methods. Land has never been unused or untouched —whether by bison, native people, or simply by nature, in the form of fire.

Teaching gardeners and others in the care of the land to simulate such natural-management strategies of American plants is a priority on the center's agenda. Through its journal, newsletter, fact sheets, and other publications, including a state-by-state list of recommended wildflowers for cultivation, NWRC helps its growing membership make a contribution to what it hopes will be an ever-larger native American landscape.

OPPOSITE: *The flower stalks of a variant of* Ipomopsis rubra, *the standing cypress, at the demonstration garden at The National Wildflower Research Center.* THIS PAGE, CLOCKWISE FROM BOTTOM: *Also displayed there are prickly poppy* (Argemone albiflora); *prairie verbena* (Verbena bipinnatifida); *purple coneflower* (Echinacea purpurea); *black Sampson* (Echinacea angustifolia); *Mexican hat* (Ratibida columnaris *or* R. columnifera); *and Texas bluebonnets* (Lupinus texensis).

JOE AND CAROLYN
OSBORN
AUSTIN, TEXAS

THERE IS NO LANDSCAPE plant more popular than turf-grass—lawn—despite all we now know about its wasteful, polluting habits. And we are as hooked on it as it is on water and chemicals. Without a lawn, the common lament goes, how do you make a landscape—and how do you make a lawn without mowable exotic grasses that guzzle resources?

Joe and Carolyn Osborn of Austin, Texas, are among a new breed of Americans who are having it both ways: They have their

A NEW AMERICAN LAWN

The Osborns have it both ways: the look of a traditional lawn, but one made of native buffalo grass (Buchloe dactyloides, *detail* BELOW) *that requires less*

mowing, watering, or fertilizing and remains green much of the growing season. The use of local stonework, TOP RIGHT AND OPPOSITE, BELOW, *adds to the natural character of the property. A trellis-covered walkway leads from the garage to the house* (RIGHT AND OPPOSITE, ABOVE).

traditional-looking lawn, but it is made up of native grasses that demand less water, fertilizer, and mowing—lawns that fit the profile of a natural habitat garden. Landscape architect Steve Domigan developed the plan for their yard, and Environmental Survey Consulting installed large-scale local rock to further enhance the natural character of the design.

The Osborns' lawn is buffalo grass (*Buchloe dactyloides*), a native plant whose range extends throughout the Great Plains states—roughly the middle third of the country and extending north to Canada and south into Mexico. It grows in alkaline, heavy clay, and other conditions.

The Osborns' buffalo grass lawn was installed as sod, which must be cut very thick to accommodate enough of the root system, making this an expensive but nearly instant method of coverage. Buffalo grass can also be installed as plugs, spaced about eight inches apart, or

seeded. However, some of the best varieties are not available as seed since they are vegetatively propagated to ensure consistency, such as all-female strains that create a denser appearance.

Now established, their buffalo grass is fertilized half the recommended amount in fall with an all-natural organic formula, and watered only as much as needed to keep it green (a twenty-minute soak two or three times a summer). If left unwatered, it will not die but will brown down to a dormant state. Although the Osborns still prefer to mow once or twice a season to keep the grass about six inches high, it can be left to grow to a somewhat shaggy foot and a half.

SALLY TAPPEN
LITTLE COMPTON,
RHODE ISLAND

THE LARGEST WETLANDS ON earth are the oceans, and yet, the land that lies along the coast is more like grassland or even dryland. Desiccating winds scrape across the shoreline, especially in winter. And scorching sun, reflected off the water, toasts unprotected plants. Sally Tappen is an accomplished and a fearless gardener, whose main passion is played out in a rock garden filled with a collection of plants arranged in a Japanese style. The rock garden is off to one side of the house—a bit protected from

LITTLE PRAIRIE
ON THE HOUSE

the harshest winds of this island off the coast of Rhode Island.

When Sally Tappen needed to enlarge her family's summer home, she built down instead of up, BELOW, NEAR RIGHT. *But not to disturb the view, she created a version of a sod roof: a prairie*

planting with grasses and even blue lupines, ABOVE, ABOVE RIGHT, *and* OPPOSITE, FAR RIGHT—*perfect for the windy oceanside site. Imagine rooms hidden beneath the prairie,* BELOW, FAR RIGHT.

The house she lives in had been a summer and occasional weekend retreat for her family for years. When it was time for her husband, David, to retire, they decided to leave New York City and live here year-round. But the house was too small. Building up above the little cottage didn't seem right. And adding wings, left or right, would have eaten up the areas where she gardens.

The solution came to her as she was reading a building magazine. "I saw a house with a sod roof, and I called the architect immediately," she recalls. "I could have my house and save the view as well. I could even make it better." They decided to build down, right into the hillside on which the cottage stands.

The view stayed the same from the windows that look out on the ocean. However, when

you walk toward the sea and gaze back at the house, you can also see a series of rooms with huge windows that face the water. Instead of sod, Tappen guessed that a kind of prairie planting of low grasses and forbs would be the right choice. In this way, she could have a handsome foreground with color through spring to fall and golden grasses that blend into the horizon in wintertime.

Drought-tolerant and wind-resistant plants such as indigo lupines and tons of butter yellow coreopsis star in the little prairie on the house. This is a planting for eye-appeal, so red clover and daisies were permitted in the mix. The plants are naturally short, but the exposure to relentless winds dwarfs them as well. Sod or, more precisely, lawn would have been impossible to maintain in what actually is a rooftop container garden. But these plants need no feeding or watering, and best of all, only a once-yearly mowing in spring.

A bit of house was ultimately added on the level of the original building. It's a living room with a tall clerestory window.

"It just seemed right to have even more chances to enjoy the unending view of the water," says Tappen. And of the colorful flowers that introduce it.

D R Y

The deserts are not worthless wastes. . . .

They are the breathing spaces of the West

and should be preserved forever.

~ JOHN C. VAN DYKE, 1901

COMPARED WITH A DESERT, OTHER DRYLAND communities may seem drenched. But anyone who has lived in, or more to the point gardened in, a California chaparral, or tried to coax life out of pockets in rocky cliffsides, knows that they are just as defined by their lack of water. Both of these, not just the desert, are examples of drylands, places that get twenty inches or less of rainfall a year. Deserts have to get by with less than ten.

The very word *desert* conjures up images of a vintage-film scene in which soldiers of the Foreign

The desert is far from a desolate place—on the contrary it teems with animal and plant life, RIGHT. *A cactus wren,* ABOVE, *the largest North American member of its family, surveys its domain from the flower spike of an agave and fills the air with its cacophonous chug chug chug chug.*

LANDS

Legion crawl toward a pool of water only to find it a cruel mirage.

In reality, a desert is hardly a wasteland, but a complex (if initially somewhat difficult to interpret) community of plants and animals. All but the harshest of our deserts teem with life: loud-mouthed cactus wrens perching on an agave flower spike, iridescent hummingbirds darting from hot-colored chuparosa to brilliant red penstemon, lizards scuttling across the griddle-hot earth without apparent discomfort, and denizens that protect themselves from the environment by appearing only at night, or not at all. America's deserts rarely conform to the Saharan cliché of pure sand and unrelenting sun. The Sonoran Desert in Arizona and Mexico, for example, has one of the world's greatest amphibian populations—a class of cold-blooded invertebrates usually associated with wetlands.

Eight percent of the nation or 300,000 square miles qualifies as true desert. North America's four major desert zones, stretching north as far as eastern Oregon and touching parts of Idaho, Wyoming, Utah, Colorado, all of Nevada, parts of California, Arizona, New Mexico, and right into southwest Texas, hardly make up a homogeneous landscape, however.

Evaporation rates also influence how dry a desert will be; dryness is influenced by temperature, wind, and other variables such as whether the sun appears on the days rainfall occurs. Elevation, too, plays a large role in dictating what grows in each of the various arid zones. For example, though rainfall is similar and both have hot summers, winter temperatures in Albuquerque can get twenty degrees colder than in Phoenix. A desert is not a desert is not a desert.

Dry places are also subject to another harsh reality: regular periods of drought—either seasonal, or longer. Months pass without any precipitation; even a five-year span is possible. Los Angeles's last drought began in 1988–89 with only 4.56 inches of rain.

In each of our home landscapes, there may be dry spots, or niches, that are much tougher on plants than almost every other place. Learning to cultivate them as such with appropriate native flora is much more sensible than insisting on planting a thirsty variety and then constantly irrigating it, wasting our own labor and the earth's resources.

The need to conserve water will increase rather than decrease as time goes on. Scientists report that much of the nation, and the planet, is facing or will be facing the realities of drought and/or a shortage of clean, fresh water in the not-so-distant future—and not just typically dry places. In Florida, where the average annual rainfall is a generous fifty-five inches, some areas are already experiencing problems with saltwater infiltrating the water supply, because of a too-great human demand.

It is heartening to see the gradual emergence of the landscape philosophy known as Xeriscaping, a system of water conservation through creative landscaping developed in 1981 by the Denver Water Department. The name was later trademarked and given to the nonprofit National Xeriscape Council of Roswell, Georgia, which serves to promote the practice. In Xeriscaping, plants are chosen not just for regional suitability, but for use in the specific microclimate being landscaped. Turf areas are planted with species adapted to the local precipitation; irrigation is provided by the most efficient method possible, or in some cases even eliminated. (Antiturf ordinances have been proposed in the desert, but have yet to succeed.) There is great wisdom in the Xeriscape approach, but in one aspect it falls short. Native plants that have evolved under local rainfall patterns are best adapted for Xeriscaping but are not always preferred. In California, in particular, gardeners concerned

An iridescent hummingbird, TOP LEFT, can always be found darting among tubular red flowers, while lizards skip across the hot desert floor, TOP RIGHT. Although the desert might be the first dryland that comes to mind, arid places exist all over the country. California coastal cliffs, LEFT, encounter desiccating winds and have little soil, resulting in equally parched conditions. The desert itself presents various environments—elevation plays a role. The low desert may have forests of tall saguaro, BELOW FAR LEFT, while the higher desert has a different vegetation due to its climate, BELOW LEFT.

Kate Wyckoff of Beach Plum Gardens in Sag Harbor, New York, points out that seaside sites compound sandy soil with high winds to create arid conditions even in regions with adequate rainfall, such as coastal Long Island, RIGHT. *Stabilizing the dunes is a difficult task. Often native dune grasses can be planted in the sand to fight erosion,* ABOVE. *Post oak* (Quercus stellata) *and eastern red cedar* (Juniperus virginiana) *are the dominant trees in this windswept site,* BELOW.

about water consumption tend to work with Mediterranean plants—although as far back as 1920 researchers warned against these incredibly successful interlopers, with their massive seedbanks and choking growth habits, which make them successful "weeds." In California's lower elevations, where most of the principal cities lie, the nonnative percentage soars as high as 75 percent. Today, Australian and South American plants are also being touted as well suited to the dry regions of North America.

In Phoenix, the situation is even more critical. In this, the largest city in the United States situated in a desert, 80 percent of the residents are from elsewhere, and too many of them brought their stereotypes of alien landscapes along with their golf clubs. Lawn sprinklers pour gallons of water onto hot pavement areas, beyond the confines of the grass, where it quickly enters the air like steam from an iron. Popular Mediterranean natives and heat-radiating still lifes of rock and gravel punctuated by a token cactus or two are not appropriate desertscapes, any more than are manicured lawns.

Residents might take note of the gardening conversion experience of Dr. Robert Breunig, director of the Desert Botanical Garden in Phoenix, who decided to remove the nonnative vegetation from his typical homesite and grow desert wildflowers instead.

"I took out the lawn and the nonnative trees," says Breunig, "and at first it looked like a lot of weeds. But when the wildflowers really started coming in, the poppies and penstemons and campanulas and so on, my neighbors said, 'What are these?'

Dryland diversity, RIGHT, TOP TO BOTTOM: *thistle sage* (Salvia carduacea); *creosote* (Larrea tridentata); *prairie verbena* (Verbena bipinnatifida). FAR RIGHT: *The low-maintenance alternative to water-wasting lawn is a Phoenix wildflower "meadow," but it will need to have aliens weeded out.*

or golden ball (*Leucaena retusa*)—none of these trees gets very big. In the Sonoran Desert, for instance, the tallest native trees are in the twenty-to-thirty-foot range, meaning that the largest cacti like the saguaros (sah-WAH-ros) get tree status, at least visually. Ocotillo (*Fouquieria splendens*) provides another sharply vertical accent, but generally little grows much above eye-level.

Drought-resistant and drought-tolerant plants are commonly known to gardeners around the country, but the desert has an even cleverer category of plants: drought-avoiders. Over time, they have developed mechanisms for not being there, or not being vulnerable, when the driest days roll around. Plants that drop their leaves in hard times and go dormant—a trait called drought-deciduous—include ocotillo and palo verde. Within five days of a rainstorm, an ocotillo that looked dead can be leafed out and green again, as if by a miracle. In another example of adaptation, many springtime wildflowers simply time themselves to bloom and fade before the dry season thwarts their procreative energy.

Some plants have devised protective coatings like powder, down, wax, or hairs on their leaves to reflect the sun and to conserve moisture. The hairy foliage of Texas silverleaf (*Leucophyllum frutescens*) comes to mind—the selection 'Texas Ranger', developed by the breeding program at Texas A&M University in Dallas, is prized for its consistent appearance. Another favorite: *Eriogonum crocatum*'s chartreuse flowers are positively breathtaking against its tiny silver leaves. Chuparosa (*Beloperone californica* or *Justicia californica*) has tiny, finely hairy gray-green

CLOCKWISE FROM TOP, LEFT: *Leguminous woody plants include shrubby fairy duster* (Calliandra californica); *and trees such as honey mesquite* (Prosopis glandulosa); *mimosa* (Acacia berlandieri); *palo verde* (Cercidium microphyllum); *golden-ball lead tree* (Leucaena retusa); *desert willow* (Chilopsis linearis).

leaves and a brilliant display of red flowers that is irresistible to hummingbirds, hence the common name that is Spanish for the tiny, highly active birds.

Part of dealing with dry times is knowing how to take best advantage of wet times, which are often not just rainstorms but deluges. The giant saguaro cactus (*Cereus giganteus* or *Carnegiea gigantea*) of the Sonoran Desert can double its weight during a rainstorm. An intricate network of spongelike roots soaks up water before it rushes away in dry steambeds called washes, or arroyos, worn into the earth by years of runoff. Although they stand thirty or forty feet tall, saguaro roots extend only a foot or less below the soil surface.

Even on the steep hillsides of the Saguaro National Monument, where runoff must be almost instantaneous, these giants stand watch between rainfalls. They can live three hundred years, it was revealed when one called "Granddaddy" died in 1992. At over forty feet tall, it had more than fifty arms. Most saguaros don't put out their first arm till they are sixty years old, and some never branch at all. At five years old, a saguaro may be only half an inch tall; by twenty, barely a foot. At thirty, it finally flowers, only at night—welcoming nectar-feeding bats who pollinate the white blooms. Fruit soon follows, attracting the many birds who appreciate its red flesh. If that were not enough, the saguaro does even more to earn its keep as part of the complex desert environment: birds like Harris's hawks nest in cavities carved up high in its trunk. A model citizen, the saguaro is a symbol of what habitat-style gardening is about.

OPPOSITE: *During rainstorms, water runs off hillsides into the arroyos, or desert washes, becoming turbulent rushing streams that disappear almost as quickly as they form. The banks are often rich with plant life because of the additional moisture. Steve Martino, one of the leading landscape architects using native plants, says, "The wash is my favorite part of the desert; it's where the action is."*
RIGHT: *A several-hundred-year-old saguaro (*Carnegiea gigantea *or* Cereus giganteus*).*

A Desert Palette

When Desert Botanical Garden was founded in 1937, the 150-acre site was dedicated to the development of a natural garden of plants representing the deserts of the world. More than half the world's cactus species and succulents from almost every arid region are represented in the vast collection, which serves as both research and the inspiration and education of desert gardeners.

The philosophy of the Phoenix public garden has from the start allowed for certain nonnative plants. But when they are recommended for landscape use outside the living archive, the criteria become much stricter to prevent possible invasion by disruptive aliens.

Potential landscape subjects must "fit the visual ecology of the area," says Robert Breunig, director of the garden. "It's a very subjective, emotional type of thing."

Aesthetics aside, though, there is one hard-and-fast rule. "We always do a lot of soul-searching before introducing anything nonnative that could be a pest," says Breunig. "You always have to be very careful."

Plants Recommended for Desert Landscapes
by the Desert Botanical Garden

Trees

Acacia schaffneri, twisted acacia

Acacia smallii, sweet acacia

Acacia willardiana, palo blanco

Celtis pallida, desert hackberry

Cercidium floridum, blue palo verde

Cercidium microphyllum, little-leaf palo verde

Cercidium praecox, palo brea

Chilopsis linearis, desert willow

Lysiloma thornberi, fern-of-the-desert

Olneya tesota, ironwood

Parkinsonia aculeata, Mexican palo verde

Pithecellobium flexicaule, Texas ebony

Prosopis veluntina, honey mesquite

Sophora secundiflora, Texas mountain laurel

Perennial Wildflowers

Baileya multiradiata, desert marigold

Melampodium leucanthum, blackfoot daisy

Oenothera spp., evening primrose

Penstemon parryi, beardtongue

Penstemon eatonii, beardtongue

Sphaeralcea ambigua, globe mallow

CLOCKWISE FROM TOP LEFT: *Golden barrel cactus* (Echinocactus grusonii); *ocotillo* (Fouquieria splendens); Agave vilmoriniana; *littleleaf cordia* (Cordia parvifolia); *a hummingbird at the Desert Botanical Garden.*

Shrubs

Atriplex lentiformis, quailbush
Baccharis sarothroides, desert broom
Caesalpinia gilliesii, yellow bird of paradise
Caesalpinia pulcherrima, red bird of paradise
Calliandra californica, Baja fairy duster
Calliandra eriophylla, fairy duster
Cassia spp., senna
Cordia parvifolia, little-leaf cordia
Dodonaea viscosa, hopbush
Encelia farinosa, brittlebush

Fouquieria splendens, ocotillo
Justicia californica, chuparosa
Justicia spicigera, hummingbird bush
Larrea tridentata, creosote
Leucophyllum frutescens, Texas ranger
Leucophyllum laevigatum, cenizo
Salvia greggii, autumn sage
Tecoma stans, Arizona yellowbell
Vauquelinia californica, Arizona rosewood

Ground Covers

Dalea greggii, trailing smokebush
Lantana montevidensis, trailing lantana

Verbena peruviana, Peruvian verbena
Verbena pulchella, verbena

Vines

Antigonon leptopus, queen's wreath
Mascagnia macroptera, yellow orchid vine

Merremia aurea, yellow morning glory vine

Succulents

Agave americana, century plant
Agave murpheyi, agave
Carnegiea gigantea, saguaro
Dasylirion wheeleri, desert spoon
Echinocereus engelmannii, hedgehog cactus
Ferocactus spp., barrel cactus
Hesperaloe parviflora, red yucca
Nolina microcarpa, beargrass

Opuntia basilaris, beavertail prickly pear
Opuntia engelmannii, prickly pear
Opuntia ficus-indica, Indian fig prickly pear
Opuntia violacea (*O. santa-rita*), purple prickly pear
Portulacaria afra, elephant bush
Yucca baccata, banana yucca
Yucca elata, soaptree
Yucca rigida, blue yucca

CLOCKWISE FROM TOP RIGHT: *Trailing smokebush* (Dalea greggii); *the garden's demonstration area;* Agave americana *and* Cercidium spp.; *bladderpod* (Cleome isomeris); *mature plantings at the garden.*

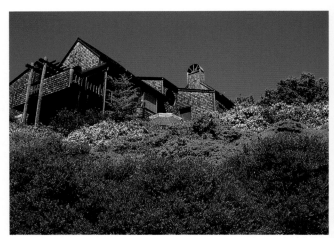

There has been some conjecture as to whether the oil-rich, alien eucalyptus tree leaves contributed to the severity of the 1991 fire in Oakland, California. According to eyewitnesses, "trees were exploding all over the place." Some slow-growing natives, on the other hand, are not strangers to fire. In fact, fire exposure is necessary for the germination of giant sequoia seeds. Xeriscaping is the rage in dryland areas, RIGHT, inspired by sites such as at the University of California, Berkeley Botanical Garden; "firescaping" is just beginning to catch on, ABOVE. Several native plants are fire-resistant or even fire-retardant, such as dwarf coyote brush (Baccharis pilularis *var*. pilularis). In general, keep dead wood and brush cleared away at all times, and select low-growing natives that remain green during seasons of greatest fire hazard, such as bearberry or kinnikinick (Arctostaphylos uva-ursi), BELOW. OPPOSITE: Colorful annuals growing with spiny agave in a Xeriscape planting.

DRYLAND TIPS

For aesthetics as well as the possibilities of shade, capitalize on bright light conditions by creating shadow pictures on the ground or on walls. Position particularly architectural plants like ocotillo, agave, and yucca so that the afternoon sun hits them most dramatically. Use the shade to expand the plant repertoire.

"Microclimate is very important in the arid environment," says landscape architect Carol Shuler of Arizona. "For example, shade pockets in the landscape can support very different plants than other spots, and what grows on the north and south side of a berm will be very different."

Sometimes, dryland landscapes need supplemental water to thrive, but it should be applied in the most efficient way possible and also at the right time. Shuler advises her clients to water well in early June, and then around midmonth, to help plants be prepared for the hottest, driest part of the season and avoid desiccation.

Professional horticulture of the desert is very young; new varieties are being released all the time. Native-plant demonstration gardens are one of the best sources for up-to-date information on the selections best suited to your region and where to obtain them.

CAROL SHULER AND
KENT NEWLAND
CAVE CREEK, ARIZONA

WHEN LANDSCAPE ARCHI-
tect Carol Shuler and botanist
Kent Newland married, it was
the beginning of a great cactus
empire: Their cherished collections merged to become one, and
now the plants share the spot-
light in the couple's outdoor
environment.

At the back of the house, the
cactus collection is like a living
sculpture garden. The bizarre,
spiny forms of the hundreds of
specimens mimic the greater
desert around them.

Sometimes, large specimens

GIFTS TO THE GARDEN

*A palo verde tree
underplanted with penstemon,*
BELOW, *grows outside the
walled entry garden, as does
the aloe hybrids collection,*
OPPOSITE. *Inside the walled*

*area at sunset, the petals of
birdcage evening primrose
(Oenothera deltoides),*
ABOVE RIGHT, *unfurl in a
matter of minutes. Kent
Newland's "collection
garden,"* TOP RIGHT,
grows in pots behind the house.

outgrow their pots and are integrated into the landscape, particu-
ularly shrubby types of prickly
pear (*Opuntia* spp.) that grow to
three to five feet tall. "Their
round pads make a nice contrast
with the other desert plants,"
says Shuler, "and they have big,
colorful flowers."

In true scientific style, Newland groups the potted cacti by
genus—all the mammillarias together, for example—on the
deck area behind the house.
When a particular plant or group
is in its flowering season, he
shifts it to a better viewing point
on the raised, stepped platform.

The cacti are as much part of
the couple's landscape plan as
their enclosed front courtyard
garden of butterfly plants, where
each evening from March to
May a family ritual centers on
the unfurling birdcage evening
primrose flowers (*Oenothera deltoides*).

Landscaping of the 1.25-acre

property with flora of the Sonoran and other nearby deserts is a
year-round family endeavor—
even at Christmastime. Each
year, a live desert tree—a screw-
bean mesquite, a sweet acacia, a
palo verde—has first acted as the
Christmas tree, and then settles
into the outdoor landscape, underplanted with muhlenbergias
and other native grasses.

Some have found their way to
prominent status in what Shuler
calls their "mesquite bosque," a
little homemade forest of *Prosopis*
species that promises to fill in
with Christmases to come.

CINDY AND STEVE
LESHIN
PARADISE VALLEY,
ARIZONA

WHY CINDY AND STEVE Leshin's Paradise Valley home is set so far back into its one-acre lot is not immediately clear, especially not to one new at desert ecology. But it is the lay of the land—of the washes, specifically, those dry streambeds through which water rushes in wet times —that is the law here. An existing wash, which cannot be altered even to build a house, determined the siting.

A few foothills palo verdes (*Cercidium microphyllum*) and old

AWASH IN COLOR

The staghorn cholla (Opuntia acanthocarpa) *has a handsome habit,* TOP RIGHT; *translucent spines,* SECOND FROM TOP; *and beautiful flowers,* THIRD FROM TOP.

Plantings, BOTTOM RIGHT AND ABOVE, *have been arranged to frame views.*
OPPOSITE: *The entrance to the property with red chuparosa* (Justicia californica), *yellow brittlebush and desert marigold, and violet* Verbena rigida.

saguaros were all there was to work with when the Leshins hired designer Carol Shuler to landscape their property more than ten years ago. Mesquites and acacias were among the trees she added to the design, in which she carefully protected a startling view of the nearby Camelback Mountain, framing it with well-placed boulders and plantings.

To contend with the awkward setback, Shuler flanked the ambling driveway with a mix of shrubs and herbaceous plants, which at its farthest edges becomes somewhat thicketlike— creating ideal cover for birds, which the Leshins had indicated was one of their top priorities. Creosote (*Larrea tridentata*), a common sight in the American desert with its olive foliage and yellow flowers, and various sculptural cacti are among the components of the area. *Atriplex lentiformis* (quailbush) brought in the quails; orioles are drawn by the aloes figured into the plan.

Today, a wildflower display of pink, coral, rust, and red desert mallows (*Sphaeralcea ambigua*), purple-flowered *Verbena rigida,* red penstemons, and fiery chuparosa (*Justicia californica*) makes the drive's edges lively spots for hummingbirds and butterflies.

Even rabbits and bees are especially appreciative of several nonliving elements: what Cindy Leshin calls "bird waterers," simply large glazed terra-cotta pot saucers sunk into the soil, leaving the lip above the surface. They are hooked into an irrigation line for replenishment, reliable oases in an unpredictable habitat.

OPPOSITE: *A young mesquite tree frames a view of the colorful plantings. Pink evening primrose* (Oenothera speciosa), LEFT, *is planted under flowering yuccas.*

ABOVE: *A wonderful trellis covers the front of the house. Landscape designer Carol Shuler sheltered the house with plantings for a sense of privacy in a setting of wide-open spaces.*

they are not feeding in the branches of the desert willow (*Chilopsis linearis*) or Arizona yellowbells (*Tecoma stans*). With only seven inches of rainfall, the Douglases' garden is nevertheless a paradise.

Plants were neither saved nor added to the site for their visual effect alone, but for their enjoyment by wildlife. Seeds of mesquite trees (*Prosopis* spp.), for instance, are favored by squirrels and by peccaries (a wild nocturnal mammal related to the pig). Perhaps most unforgettable are a number of centuries-old saguaro cacti (*Carnegiea gigantea* or *Cereus giganteus*) that stand guard over the place, at thirty feet or more

at once sentinels and combination birdhouses-feeders.

Less evident are the baby saguaros. Cliff Douglas gestures to a visitor to come closer and share the secret, bending down to poke around under a bur sage. There, in the protective custody of the shrub, is a tiny saguaro.

"I've been watching this one for five years," says Douglas.

LEFT: *Tinted stucco walls offer a colorful foil for sunlight and foliage.* ABOVE: *A curved wall contains a planting and borders the walk to the front door.* OPPOSITE: *Viewed from the other direction, this destination is seen through an ocotillo.*

ABOVE: *Ground covers— silvery camphor dune tansy* (Tanacetum camphoratum), *native to San Francisco, and sea fig* (Carpobrotus chilensis) *from Baja.* OPPOSITE: *Faded fronds of the California fan palm* (Washingtonia filifera) *persist to cover trunks.*

BOTANISTS CONCERNED WITH conserving native flora often lament that California is already a lost cause. Of the nearly 3,000 plant species that are threatened or endangered in the United States, 680 are Californian, and a frightening share of the state's current flora is exotic. However,

CULTIVATED PRESERVATION

the commitment of many residents to their indigenous flora is equal to their legendary love of the great outdoors—the California Native Plant Society is probably the most active in the nation.

Rancho Santa Ana Botanic Garden was founded in 1927 by Susanna Bixby Bryant. It is primarily a botanical research and educational institution, offering a

graduate degree in botany. The director, Dr. Thomas S. Elias, is one of the investigators into sources of the anticancer drug taxol, now made from the western yew and its relatives.

Conservation is another aim of the garden. Members believe that such facilities are like the best zoos of the world: repositories of endangered species as a small step toward stopping extinction. Fortunately, plant breeding in a simulated environment is usually easier than with such animals as the California condor, though not without risks.

The collection, which moved from historic Rancho Santa Ana in Orange County to Claremont in 1951, has grown to be not just a living catalog of southern California plants, but coincidentally also one of water-wise garden

plants. Nearly 40 percent of the state's precious water supply is used outdoors, in the landscape. Now, the testing, development, and promotion of natives for landscape use will become a major goal. Sophisticated seed collecting and storing, sowing, and growing techniques have yielded one hundred natives never before seen in cultivation, and nursery areas are being enlarged to support this effort; nearly sixty new ornamentals have been introduced by the garden to the nursery trade.

In the California Cultivars Garden, the rolling lawn at the entrance isn't grass at all but low-growing manzanitas (*Arctostaphylos* cultivars) selected for drought-tolerance and eye-appeal. Elsewhere, native Douglas irises, which vary in nature, have been selected for flower size and color, proving to home gardeners that

there can be as much beauty in rugged natives as in ornamental exotics. California lilacs (*Ceanothus* spp.) figure prominently because of their profuse blue flowers, but are important landscape and wildlife plants, too, producing needed cover and berries. Low-growers prevent erosion and reduce loss of soil moisture; taller ones make good screens. Fremontias (*Fremontodendron* spp.), the state shrub, and Oregon grape hollies (*Mahonia* spp.) are also cultivated and promoted.

The cacti and succulents on the eighty-six-acre grounds, usually attract the most attention—except, perhaps, for the ever-present scurrying lizards. Most plants here bloom in early spring, following late-winter rains, and quickly attract pollinators and set seed before the hot, dry season begins.

ABOVE LEFT: *Douglas iris* (Iris douglasiana) *at the lower pool.* ABOVE RIGHT: *The state flower, California poppy* (Eschscholzia californica). OPPOSITE, LEFT TO RIGHT, TOP TO BOTTOM: *California's state shrub, flannel bush* (Fremontodendron californicum); Aristolochia californica; Heuchera maxima; *California blue-eyed grass* (Sisyrinchium bellum); *coastal tidytips* (Layia platyglossa); *hedgehog cactus* (Echinocereus *spp.*).

MANY DRYLAND PLANTS, much like the brilliant alpine meadow flora, burst into bloom at the earliest chance in spring to attract pollinators, set seeds or fruit, and quickly wrap them in tightly sealed pods—"frozen" until the next moment of moisture appears.

Kevin Connelly of Arcadia, California, has learned from the plants how to take advantage of wet times in dry places, too, and following their cues he has made wildflower gardens since 1975.

IN THE COMMUNITY SPIRIT

OPPOSITE: *One of California's many legumes, Bentham's or spider lupine* (Lupinus benthamii), *native to Los Angeles, presents a cascade of blue flowers among*

other showy natives such as deep pink owl's clover (Orthocarpus purpurascens var. ornatus) *on a hillside.*
ABOVE: *Sea dahlia* (Coreopsis maritima) *is a perennial native of coastal southern California.*

At Earthside Nature Center, a two-acre garden only for natives founded in 1971, Connelly and naturalist-author Elna Bakker work with more than color combinations in mind. Though the place is positively brilliant, what was first in the gardeners' minds was a desire to see plants with their natural companions.

To that end, desert bluebells (*Phacelia campanularia*), desert dandelions (*Malacothrix glabrata*), and pink lupines (*Lupinus arizonicus*) conjure up images of the Colorado desert washes they all hail from. In a section of the garden devoted to coastal species, the medley is blue-violet *Phacelia parryi,* red-violet *Lupinus hirsutissimus* and *Salvia leucophylla*—beautiful, but also true to nature.

The two-acre site is mostly flat, but at the edge of it, pathways zigzag down a dry hillside of many small plantings, some punctuated by succulents. Tidytips (*Layia platyglossa*), blue-eyed Mary (*Collinsia verna*), baby

WET

What would the world be, once bereft

Of wet and wildness? Let them be left,

O let them be left, wildness and wet;

Long live the weeds and the wildness yet.

~ GERARD MANLEY HOPKINS

EVERY HABITAT IS DEFINED BY WATER. EVEN the harshest desert is described in terms of water's scarcity. Wetlands—places where water is relatively plentiful for all or part of the year—are among the earth's most productive ecosystems in terms of biological output (of both plant and animal life) for two reasons: because the sun's energy is stored by the water, and because in most wetlands, decomposition is quite efficient, so "used" materials get broken down and recycled quickly.

That wetlands rival the richest farmlands in productivity is hardly what the American government was saying when it passed down the order to "re-

In spring, swamp pink (Helonias bullata), ABOVE, *shoots up a flower from a flat basal rosette. It is endangered because its habitat is vanishing.* RIGHT: *The vernal pool at Tower Hill Botanic Garden usually dries up by summer, but some years it's still wet through fall.*

LANDS

claim" 65 million wet acres in the middle of the last century. Draining wetlands to make farmland or some other "productive" form of acreage was a misguided mandate of our emerging nation, a policy that some estimates say led to the loss of more than half the wetlands that existed when the settlers arrived in what is now the United States. A 1992 estimate, more conservative but nevertheless dismal, set the figure at 99 million acres lost from an original total of 240 million.

Despite our heightened awareness of wetlands, they remain our most imperiled habitats. In the late 1980s, various environmental groups placed the annual rate of loss at anywhere from 300,000 acres to as much as half a million (at the same time the federal government was promising, in 1988, no net loss).

Beyond the numbers, the word *swamp* is still far from summoning up images of a diverse wet woodland with exquisitely rich soil, instead of a mosquito breeding ground. Someday a prospective homeowner may gaze upon the low, damp spot in his new backyard and say "My dream bog garden come true!" but it is still more often "Bring in the bulldozer!" Incorporating water into our landscapes can serve as an object lesson for all of us, though, and will begin to make us all champions of wetlands.

"Rather than 'wastelands,' wetlands are really wonderlands," says JoAnn Gillespie, proprietor of Country Wetlands Nursery in Muskego, Wisconsin, who has been committed to the cause of these fragile and misunderstood systems for more than fifteen years. "The [wetland] plants aren't endangered," she says. "The ecosystems are."

The grassy marshlands, RIGHT, *are disappearing at an alarming rate. Wetlands, among the most threatened habitats, are prime for exploitation: They are flat, which is good for development; have great recreational possibilities; and are filled with resources such as edible species and water itself. But the tide is beginning to turn.*

Until relatively recently it was virtually open season on wetlands. Even in the "enlightened" years of regulation, it appears that still almost no one really wants one in his or her own backyard—the nursery business for wetland plants is in its infancy, far behind the rest of the nursery trade. Ed Garbisch of Environmental Concern, St. Michaels, Maryland, whose industry-leading firm has undertaken 350-plus large-scale wetlands projects, says that virtually all of them were performed because the law required that the landowner do so. "Only four of three hundred fifty projects in twenty years were voluntary restorations," he reports.

These great living systems make life possible. Some contribute to the water table, helping recharge groundwater reserves; others filter pollutants or remove sediment, mediate floods, and perform many other feats we too often fail to appreciate. That ignorance simply must change.

"We need to think of wetlands as amenities, not aggravations," says Michael Hollins, a wetlands ecologist from Envirens, Inc., in Freeland, Maryland. Indeed, too many landscapers and builders still drain wet areas or level them with fill rather than delighting in them as is.

"I do not do my gardening beside a marsh, or even have a pond," you may be saying, but no matter. This chapter is for every gardener, since each of us thinking of landscaping in the habitat style must commit to including water in his or her design. The smallest elements, mere mud puddles and water collected under a downspout, or a little homemade garden pool, can help in at least a token way to begin to reconnect the cycle of life in a place that is otherwise sadly incomplete. Even when it's accomplished in anything but a scientific manner—a brimming stock tank of waterlilies beside the barn—water works.

When a plan for a garden is begun, professionals start with what is called "the program." It is simply the needs and desires of the people who will use the landscape. Some might assign space for a swing set or a barbecue pit top priority, but for me it was a water feature. The presence of water, particularly when combined with cover and an abundance of fruiting plants, makes even my tough city lot attractive to wildlife and gives the garden a habitat character it would not otherwise possess.

TOP LEFT: *Wetlands are wonderlands, not wastelands.* CENTER: *A small waterfall in the Scanlon garden in Texas. Every bit of water brings sights, sounds, and birds. This simple ornamental cistern,* RIGHT, *at Skylands, the New Jersey State Botanical Garden in Ringwood, is a welcome stopping place for birds.*

My pool is home to my exotic fish called Koi—a kind of carp bred by the Japanese from German and Asian stock. Today, I might not recommend stocking even an isolated pool with such exotic creatures, but I think of my fish as a collection, the way another person might collect hostas.

Introducing these fish, however pretty and responsive to human attention that they are, to a wild pond or stream would be a disaster, since they root around the bottom, stirring up muck and clouding the water, which can damage the environment for other fish.

Even though my pool is anything but a natural wetland—it has a PVC liner and a pump and filter—it is the pulse of the garden. The fish gobble insects, the water is home to frogs, and a favorite place for birds—many more species and numbers than are attracted to any neighborhood bird feeder in any season. Toads, too, have found the moist, rocky edges of the pool, and eat slugs and other pests.

I have found a source for native fish, and would like to try some. In the future, I would limit the

TOP LEFT: *Turtlehead* (Chelone lyonii) *is a herbaceous plant that loves the streamside.* CENTER: *Living things abound, and frequent inhabitants include amphibians, such as this toad.* RIGHT: *Stepping-stones span a pool made with a plastic liner that graces a central Texas garden.*

plants around the pool to species that would be found in a wet environment in Brooklyn. There must have been plenty, the Dutch having named it "broken land" for its patchwork of wet and dry places. Already, I have some moisture-loving native Americans in my repertory, with buttonbush (*Cephalanthus occidentalis*), cardinal flower (*Lobelia cardinalis*), bog rosemary (*Andromeda glaucophylla*), jack-in-the-pulpit (*Arisaema triphyllum*), marsh marigold (*Caltha palustris*), ferns, and mosses among them. I have never had much luck with waterlilies (the carp like them, too), but there are handsome native species to be grown, including the fragrant one (*Nymphaea odorata*). (A fuller complement of water and wetland plants appears later in this section.)

For those whose gardens are larger than twenty-one by fifty feet, wetland-simulation plans can be even more ambitious. Start by analyzing all the potential water resources on the property: the rain and melted snow that run off the roof, the sump area where excess moisture is collected, even those depressions in the yard that simply never drain well after a shower. A large piece of land with a storm-water pond would make an ideal wetland garden.

Craig Tufts, director of the backyard wildlife habitat program of the National Wildlife Federation, is a

good model for wetlands gardening. Instead of watching all the roof runoff at his suburban Virginia homesite flow wastefully across the lawn and into the curbside drains, Tufts created his own little marsh.

Someday, Tufts says, he'll live next to a real marsh. In the meantime, he's enjoying the added dimension his homemade minimarsh has brought—large numbers of butterflies "mudpuddling" on the moist soil, a wider diversity of birds, and amphibians, too, plus the potential to grow wet-loving plants like pickerel-weed (*Pontederia cordata*), sweet pepperbush (*Clethra alnifolia*), wafer ash (*Ptelea trifoliata*), and silky dog-wood (*Cornus amomum*) to name just a few.

The process of creating the marsh was no more difficult than preparing for a perennial border or any other new garden area. After deciding the outline and location, Tufts lifted the sod (about 450 square feet of it) and excavated down to just over a foot deep.

To one of the downspouts from his gutter system, he connected a piece of flexible plastic pipe so that the water could be directed down and away from the house, via a ditch, into the top of the marsh basin. He had to experiment with the angle and the position of the pipe after the first few rainstorms, and he back-filled with clay to slow downward percolation, until the moisture-holding capacity of the basin and the movement of water from the pipe were what he wanted.

Then, using a tiller on the site he mixed up some "marsh soil"—lots of peat, some sand, compost, and much of the original subsoil he had excavated, and

ABOVE: *A well-tuned New England pond in autumn includes various life-forms, from tiny bacteria and microscopic animals to the cattails at the water's edge. Wetland meets woodland,* OPPOSITE. *The places where habitats meet, in this case the riparian edge, are often where the most complex communities flourish.*

lined the uneven basin with an even layer of this mix so that some areas remained deeper than others. Rainwater no longer washes across a useless lawn to become part of the sewer system; it moves slowly "downstream" toward a handsome stand of Joe-pye weed, which blooms in late summer.

Tufts chose to create a wet place by using roof runoff; for other gardeners, a good moisture supply already exists in the soil. Particularly in the East, a seasonally moist or low-lying field may become a wet meadow. Wild irises, Turk's-cap lilies, cardinal flowers, and milkweeds are just a few of the many colorful plants that would thrive under these conditions. Likewise, certain woodland environments are damp enough to support plants classified as wetland species. If water moves through your property in the form of a brook or stream, or if a pond already exists, you are among the luckiest ones. Some examples of

wet meadows and wet forests will be seen later in this chapter to help you determine if such an opportunity is hidden on your property.

Even when a natural wetland exists, there may be work to be done, too—what would be called enhancement in the wetlands business, gently helping the system to achieve a better state of health. No action should be taken without prior investigation, however; always consult with a wetlands professional and read local guidelines first.

Kate Tyree of Watermill, Long Island, developed two ponds on what were unproductive low, sodden parts of her property. When the land had been developed, the disturbance created had favored a number of weed species, and she wanted to correct that at least in part. Her motivation was to create a beautiful, healthy water garden in areas that were choked with invasive exotics.

PLANTS FOR WET PLACES

Many thousands of distinct species of plants are associated with wetland systems, including a large share that adapt to wet, medium, or even dry soil. Some of my favorite shrubs are on that list, including sweet pepperbush (*Clethra alnifolia*), with fragrant white midsummer flowers and good gold fall color. The form 'Rosea' has pink flowers. Few plants can rival the autumn display of Virginia sweetspire (*Itea virginica*), with fragrant late spring flowers and then a fiery red autumn look. The selection 'Henry's Garnet' is especially brilliant.

The swamp azalea (*Rhododendron viscosum*) is another wet-soil winner, with very fragrant white springtime blooms. Inkberry (*Ilex glabra*) makes dark blue-black fruit in fall and is pleasingly evergreen. Its relative, winterberry (*Ilex verticillata*), is a deciduous holly and serves up bright red fruit. The berries of highbush blueberry (*Vaccinium corymbosum*) are followed by a red fall foliage show and finally by a glowing red cast that the new canes take on in winter. *Cephalanthus occidentalis,* buttonbush, is a delight when in flower, producing odd ball-shaped creamy blossoms about an inch in diameter. The flowers of the sweet bay magnolia (*Magnolia virginiana*) are creamy white with a citrusy fragrance, and are followed by bright red seeds in fall.

Blue flowers are among the gardener's most treasured subjects, and in moist places there are many standouts. Perhaps no genus produces more remarkably blue blossoms than the gentians (*Gentiana* spp.). These late-blooming herbaceous perennials—great season-extenders for the native garden that seem almost immune to frost—do well in moist soil.

About the most common, and easiest to grow, is the closed or bottle gentian, *Gentiana andrewsii,* with flowers that appear to be perpetually in bud. They never open, but a tiny hole at the tip permits entry by pollinators.

Great lobelia (*Lobelia siphilitica*) is the tall blue-flowered cousin of cardinal flower (*L. cardinalis*), each among the most desirable flowering perennials of wet places, including wooded riverbanks, marshes, and wet meadows.

Another choice blue-flowered plant is pickerel rush or pickerelweed (*Pontederia cordata*), a denizen of slowly moving water. Pickerelweed, which creates thick colonies of spear-shaped foliage, also does well in a pond or pool; it can be confined in a bucket or tub. The long-blooming, skyward-pointing floral spikes give a decided vertical emphasis to the water garden.

Many other water plants might be called architectural, and could be grown as much, if not more, for their foliage than for their flowers. Though each flower may last a day or two, the forceful swordlike foliage of the iris family is present throughout the growing season. Most gardeners know German iris or Siberian iris, but the northern hemisphere is rich with iris species, including many outstanding native Americans that rarely appear as horticultural subjects. Louisiana and California, in particular, have fine native species.

A familiar iris is blue flag or wild iris (*Iris versicolor*), which grows from two to three feet high in full sun in moist soil, and even adapts to partial shade along the edges where forest meets wet meadow. In the northeastern quarter of the country, its lavender, violet, blue-violet, red-violet, or (rarely) white flowers are a familiar May-to-July sight in wet meadows. A similar species, *I. prismatica,* has grasslike foliage and is a bit shorter. The red or copper iris (*I. fulva*) is found blooming in late spring from Illinois to Georgia.

Acorus, or sweet flag, a member of the arum family, also bears irislike foliage. It has an insignificant brown spadix, a fleshy floral spike containing hundreds of tiny flowers. The species has little to recommend it as an ornamental, but a variegated selection, *Acorus calamus* 'Variegata', with

ABOVE, LEFT TO RIGHT: *Closed or bottle gentian* (Gentiana andrewsii); *sweet bay* (Magnolia virginiana); *great blue lobelia* (Lobelia siphilitica). LEFT: *Fall interest from swamp rose mallow at Rock Rim Ponds in New York;* RIGHT: *Seed pod detail.*

vertical creamy yellow stripes against grass green, is striking.

Most arums have spathes (covering hoods) like a jack-in-the-pulpit (*Arisaema triphyllum*) and are happy in wet areas. There is a native calla lily, *Calla palustris* or water arum. (The tropical plants called calla lilies are in the genus *Zantedeschia*.)

The very early blooming skunk cabbage (*Symplocarpus foetidus*) has a ruddy brown hood that completely engulfs the spadix and moderates temperatures inside, though snow may still cover the ground. The interior temperatures may be as high as seventy degrees, a factor that appeals to pollinators. The skunk cabbage is better known for its large, fleshy green leaves—a true sign of the American spring. The distinctive epithet relates to the smelly nature of the leaves when crushed. Unbruised, the leaves have no malodorous drawback to dissuade gardeners. The large, waxy hood of the western skunk cabbage, *Lysichiton americanum,* recommends it as an ornamen-

tal and appears in midspring before the giant elliptical leaves unfurl.

By contrast, the golden club (*Orontium aquaticum*) has no spathe at all, just a pollen-covered spadix. In the early spring, the plant appears as a cluster of white candles dipped in bright yellow paint. Soon, waxy green leaves sprout around them that are completely water-repellent.

Some of the arums have characteristic arrow-shaped leaves. Arrow arum (*Peltandra virginica*), so called for its attractive, fifteen-inch-tall foliage that grows from a rhizome without stems or branching, imparts a tropical feeling to a watery planting.

Arrowhead (*Sagittaria latifolia*) has edible tubers that were cultivated by Native Americans as food, and is also one of the most handsome species for an aquatic habitat garden. Complementing its shiny foliage, spikes of showy white three-petaled flowers with yellow anthers are produced midsummer to fall.

Lizard's tail (*Saururus cernuus*) could be grown for its

lush, spade-shaped foliage but also boasts curious fuzzy flower spikes that lend its descriptive common name. Peltandra, sagittaria, and saururus like to grow covered with about a foot of water.

At one time, a trip to a bog or marsh, the drainage ditch along a roadside, or beneath a bridge would have revealed exceptional flowering plants, and even today you may sight the garden-worthy *Chelone* spp. (turtle-head) or the gaudy flowers of *Hibiscus moscheutos* (swamp mallow). More often than not, however, you'll come upon acres of *Phragmites australis,* or giant reed, a plant with worldwide distribution that unfortunately takes advantage of many wet situations, particularly in disturbed areas, and chokes out everything else. An even more noxious plant, an alien, never fails to elicit as many oohs and aahs from the uninitiated as a fireworks display. The plant that has supplanted most other wet wildings in northern sunny places is purple loosestrife (*Lythrum salicaria*).

In the 1980s growers

claimed that the hybrids sold on the commercial market were sterile (and I showed them in *The Natural Garden*), but apparently some hybrids produce pollen viable enough to cross with wild stands and create even more tenacious offspring. It is disappointing to see the plant for sale in a nursery today, but even worse to see it in the border of a gardener who should know better.

Some plants called loosestrife, however, such as fringed loosestrife (*Lysimachia ciliata*), have gardenworthiness and far less potential for disaster. *L. ciliata*'s pretty yellow flowers last for several weeks, but what's best is the maroon-leaved selection, *L. c. purpurea,* a colorful foliar accent for the damp garden or native border.

This summary of the beauties of the wet would be incomplete without a mention of a particular favorite of mine, swamp or red milk-weed (*Asclepias incarnata*). It is an essential in the repertory of every habitat gardener with a moist spot—gorgeous, and an important butterfly host plant, too.

ABOVE, LEFT TO RIGHT: *Indian pond lily* (Nuphar polysepalum); *western skunk cabbage* (Lysichiton americanum); *marsh marigold* (Caltha palustris). LEFT: *Hardy water canna* (Thalia dealbata). RIGHT: *Arrowhead* (Sagittaria latifolia).

She could simply have cleared out the unwanted plants, including lots of multiflora rose, and encouraged the "keepers" from among the existing wildings, but she went a step further and also excavated to create the ponds. She then encouraged the natural plant cover from sedges (*Carex* spp.) and rushes (*Juncus* spp.) and moisture-loving shrubs like winterberry (*Ilex verticillata*), which also provides wildlife food in the form of berries.

By opening up the space and making the ponds, mosquito and fly populations have been reduced. Air circulation is better, and more animals seem to be able to make use of the area. A functioning wetland, with a system of insect and animal predation intact, will not be an insect breeding ground. Stocking the ponds helped, since fish feed on the bug population while also attracting hungry herons and the like.

Besides maximizing food and cover from natural features, Tyree erected man-made houses for the birds. She and her neighbors, who have followed Tyree's lead and created ponds on their properties—now there are five in the immediate area—have had

ABOVE: *One of America's most versatile and beautiful shrubs, winterberry* (Ilex verticillata), *revealed by Kate Tyree to best advantage.* RIGHT: *Tyree also capitalized on the wet lowland behind her house by scooping out two ponds—linked by a waterway, spanned by a bridge.*

UP WITH
INSECTS

The most evolved form of
wildlife gardening is gardening to lure insectivores, designing your landscape
deliberately to attract spi-
ders, birds, and small mammals like bats, moles, and
shrews along with toads,
frogs, and fish (the latter, of
course, only where feasible).
Once you begin to appreciate the workings of the food
chain, as the savvy insecti-
vore gardener does, planting
for a continuous bug buffet
will be far from repellent,
and instead seem the most
natural way to garden.
Without insects, there is no
food chain, without the food
chain no life. Suddenly pollen plants, nectar plants, and
host plants (the preferred
diet of larval forms of various moths and butterflies)
start to head your list of
desirables.

Someone ought to rewrite
the books on plants for wildlife so they list the plants
that insects prefer. Perhaps
prairie ecologist Neil
Diboll says it best: "Like
birds?" he quips. "Then
you better get used to bugs."

the good fortune of attracting aerobatic troupes of purple martins. Catalogs offer multiple-dwelling martin houses, promising that they're a sure thing for attracting these voracious insect-eaters. But Tyree knows the most important element to lure and keep these special swallows is water.

The gardener's role in the protection or development of the wetland habitat could be seen as an unnatural intervention. Yet wetlands are often in varying states of transition, evolving because of weather, changes in the water table, human impact (pollution, dredging, etc.), and even a natural element like fire, which affects certain wet systems, too.

Some wetlands are only seasonally wet—flooded in the spring, for example, and then dry in the warmer months. At Tower Hill Botanic Garden in Massachusetts, a wildlife garden was created around a seasonal wetland, technically called a vernal pool, where red maples dominate the magical low-lying point in the landscape where the wet meadow meets the forest.

Some wetlands are freshwater, others salt; some have currents, some tides, and in still others the water moves very little.

With all these disparate qualities, it is difficult to define wetland simply. Many professional organizations, from the Army Corps of Engineers to each recent presidential administration, have offered versions. Generally accepted is this one: wetlands are places where the soil is saturated at least seven consecutive days a year, and/or where the water table comes within a foot of the surface and stays there for seven days a year. In other words, wetlands are all around us.

OPPOSITE, ABOVE: *A familiar "good guy," daddy longlegs.* BELOW: *Purple martins are attracted to bird-apartment dwellings placed near water. They consume countless mosquitoes.* LEFT: *Fern crosiers and skunk cabbages—spring in the wetland at Garden in the Woods.*

CARNIVOROUS PLANTS

Some plants grow in places where the soil is so acidic and nutritionally poor that they have evolved other ways to get nourishment to survive. Carnivorous, or meat-eating, plants live on insects. Many are native Americans, from the Venus flytrap (*Dionaea muscipula*) of the Carolinas to the cobra lily (*Darlingtonia californica*) of the West Coast. Only 3 percent of their habitat in the United States remains.

Carnivorous plants have specialized attracting and trapping mechanisms that make them good hunters. Some stalk and snare passively: pitcher plants (*Sarracenia* spp.), for example, have vaselike leaves lined with downward-facing hairs. Victims finding their way into this "pitcher" cannot turn back and eventually make their way to a pool of water collected at the bottom, where they drown. Others are active, like the sundews (*Drosera* spp.), which react to contact with prey by actually moving. The best-known active hunter is the Venus flytrap, a "steel-trap" type plant. Carnivorous plants also have the means of digesting what they catch—with the aid of bacteria, enzymes, or both.

Flytraps and cobra lilies sold as little hothouse novelties don't make good houseplants. Most have a requirement for winter dormancy, and want more humidity than an average home can provide. Climate-controlled terrarium collections are a possibility with the cobra lilies, but they do best in outdoor bog gardens in northern California, Oregon, and British Columbia.

The carnivorous plants that hold the most promise for home habitat gardeners are the pitcher plants. Among the species to consider are pale pitcher (*Sarracenia alata*), yellow pitcher (*S. flava*), white trumpet (*S. leucophylla*), and the naturally occurring subspecies northern pitcher (*S. purpurea* subspp. *purpurea*) and southern pitcher (*S. purpurea* subspp. *venosa*).

The sarracenias hybridize freely—constantly pushing the boundaries of evolution. A collection of *Sarracenia leucophylla* will soon exhibit variations in leaf color and flower as surface-sown seeds sprout and grow. This white trumpet looks delicate with its tubular leaf, flared and hooded at the top and etched with red and green veins. This plant, little-known to American horticulture despite its native status, is grown as a popular cut flower. Actually, it's the leaves that are used. This is the species to try in Zones 7 and south. *S. flava* is alleged to be hardy in Zone 7, too,

TOP TO BOTTOM: *A fading autumn leaf (pitcher) of the yellow pitcher plant or huntsman's-horn* (Sarracenia flava); S. flava *with flowers; southern pitcher plant* (S. purpurea subspp. venosa) *in a dense planting at the Atlanta Botanical Garden.* OPPOSITE: *The northern pitcher plant* (S. purpurea subspp. purpurea). OVERLEAF: *A marshy field of blue flag iris* (Iris versicolor) *and cinnamon ferns* (Osmunda cinnamomea) *in Rhode Island.*

but it grows happily at Garden in the Woods in Framingham, Massachusetts, in Zone 5. (In severe climates enthusiasts report that they mulch with straw and pine needles and boughs up to a foot thick over winter.) Right up into Zone 3, the hardiest candidate is *S. purpurea* subspp. *purpurea,* named for its flower color though its leaves, too, are tinged purple.

If their needs are met, pitchers are not hard to grow in a boggy site, natural or man-made. Keep the crowns at the surface, above the normal water level, and give them sun—six hours or more in the north, a bit less in the south, where they will tolerate some shade. Generally speaking, grow them in an acid medium like sphagnum moss, or sphagnum mixed with peat. *Sarracenia purpurea* subspp. *purpurea* is more tolerant of a pH closer to neutral than the rest, which may prefer a mix of sphagnum and peat with one fifth coarse sand. Water with collected rain, and don't worry about fertilizer —they won't need any.

Pitcher plants can be increased by division once you have a stand of your own, or from seed, and I am encouraged to see that some native-plant nurseries are growing them ethically this way to offer to gardeners. Kim Hawks of Niche Gardens nursery in Chapel Hill, North Carolina, for example, has obtained seed from curator Rob Gardner of nearby North Carolina Botanical Garden and is offering both *purpurea* and a variable mixed species with genes from *flava, leucophylla,* and *purpurea* for a vivid display.

GRASSY PLANTS FOR THE WET

Many grasses are adapted to regions of the country with hot, dry summers like the prairies, but there are grasses for wet areas in gardens, too. Salt-marsh cockspur (*Echinochloa wateri*), variegated manna grass (*Glyceria aquatica* 'Variegata'), variegated ribbon grass or gardener's garters (*Phalaris arundinacea* 'Picta'), and fowl meadow grass (*Poa palustris*) are among them, and another is an important wildlife food and favorite of human gourmets—*Zizania aquatica* (wild rice).

Often, though, what look like grasses in the wet are really sedges, rushes, or other plants. Grasses have round, hollow stems with solid joints. Rushes, too, have cylindrical stems, but sedges have angular ones, hence the naturalist's mnemonic "Sedges have edges, rushes are round." As their uses for home landscapes are explored, many of these will certainly become important ornamentals, but perhaps their greatest asset, especially in the wetlands, is as food and cover for wildlife.

Rushes are members of the *Juncaceae* family, and although numerous plants are called rushes, they frequently turn out to be sedges—another example of why common names fall short. Several true rushes, members of the genus *Juncus,* are attractive in flower: *Juncus tenuis* (path rush), a swampland species, has full flowerheads with graceful bracts on two-foot plants. *J. gerardii* (black grass) is from the salt marsh, with magenta flowers and fruits that make it appear brown from afar.

Sedges are members of the *Cyperaceae* family. They have very ornamental flowerheads that are formed like umbrellas above triangular stems, particularly apparent among plants in the genus *Cyperus.* The *Scirpus* genus, which includes bulrushes, encompasses beautiful grass-like plants.

Carex is the sedge genus that shows the most promise for future home landscapes. I have seen carex growing by the woodland edge in Pennsylvania, some deep in shade in Illinois, and still another in full sun in Texas, where it was used as the dominant plant in a deerproof garden.

The tussock sedge (*Carex stricta*) is just what it sounds like: a big hummock, or tuft, of a plant—a handsome specimen, and unforgettable en masse. A sedge meadow during the relatively dry season may appear as a humpty-dumpty terrain. The fresh growth emerges each spring when the water is high, but because it is produced on top of the tussock, it is spared from "drowning."

I have seen eleocharis growing in drainage ditches by the Ithaca, New York, airport and in a roadside trench alongside a bluestem prairie in Austin, Texas, but this same plant is sold for a pretty penny in water-garden catalogs. *Eleocharis acicularis* (spike rush, or fiber-optic plant, in California) is a favorite grassy plant.

Cotton grass (*Eriophorum virginicum*), another sedge, has wonderful woolly puffs above straight stems. Cattails (*Typha* spp.) also form cottony masses when their seedheads ripen. Besides making fine wildlife food, they are favorite nesting perches for the red-winged blackbird, which attaches its nest to last year's flower-stalks.

ABOVE: *Soft-stem bulrush* (Scirpus validus); *sedges in rows at Country Wetlands Nursery.* RIGHT: *A great blue heron takes off in the marsh.* OPPOSITE, ABOVE: *Giant reed* (Phragmites australis); OPPOSITE, BELOW, *Nursery owner JoAnn Gillespie's license plate.*

WETLAND TIPS

Relatively few wetland restoration firms work on the residential scale—as a rule, they talk in square miles, and wear scuba gear when they work.

But you don't need fancy equipment to plant a home-sized wet meadow, or make a small water garden with an inground plastic liner, soft or rigid. Restoring a large submerged wetland or developing the littoral zone, or wet edge, can be more rigorous, but even these can be undertaken by gardeners.

To increase the wildlife potential of a pond by developing its edge plantings, what Country Wetlands Nursery of Wisconsin calls aquascaping, keep these considerations in mind:

Determine the appropriate plantings by noting the size of the pond—its open area and water depth. Observe the contours of the edge and slope toward the water. What is the water course; how often does it flood; how long do areas remain submerged? What is the nature of the soil? What plants are there now?

Only use native, noninvasive plants. That means that although giant reed (*Phrag-mites australis*) is indigenous, it is too aggressive to introduce. Never use purple loosestrife (*Lythrum salicaria*) or reed canary grass (*Phalaris arundinacea*), either. If you want cattails, for wildlife food value, remember that they can get out of hand.

Use started plants for residential applications; seeding is much slower and can frustrate the beginner.

Check purchased nursery stock carefully. Too many growers ship wetland plants covered with undesirable hitchhikers, like duckweed (*Lemna* spp.). Rinse the plants before introducing them.

Plant sparsely. Wetland plants are great colonizers. Use a diversity of species, and plant the way nature does with several of one kind in clusters, not rows.

Plant the higher ground first as a hedge against settlement and instability of the edge soil. After these are established, there will be less danger of losing plants placed closer to the water.

In spring, remove undesirables when young and easy to grab. In fall, cut off and discard seedheads of undesirables before they ripen and blow around.

The meadow is perhaps most beautiful in mid- to late summer—a time when flower gardens have usually passed their prime. TOP: *Cup plant flowers turn to equally ornamental seedheads.* CENTER: *The cardinal flower's cousin, great blue lobelia* (Lobelia siphilitica). BOTTOM: *Joe-pye weed and cup plant* (Eupatorium maculatum *and* Silphium perfoliatum).

australis) are in active growth, since neither of these important members of the community can tolerate mowing.

A third, and final, mowing is undertaken in mid-May to cut the pathways that allow visitors to move through the planting.

If it weren't mowed (or burned—not the easiest thing to accomplish in the middle of a city environment), the meadow would begin to evolve into woodland. A meadow is a transitional community, and human maintenance—in this case mowing—is what stops the natural succession from proceeding, by preventing young woody plants from getting a hold on the area.

Sometimes, exceptions have to be made in the schedule to accommodate unexpected developments in the meadow itself. The use of heavy mowing machinery season after season has resulted in some areas of soil compaction, for instance, which must be addressed and not aggravated further. And in recent years a parasitic plant called dodder, which looks like a tangle of orange string, has invaded the area, threatening the desirable plants. In order to eliminate the dodder, which twines around a host plant and intercepts food and water from its tissues, the gardeners have been mowing less and doing more hand cutting to eradicate it. All debris is removed during this period, because so much of it contains dodder, too.

By August the wet meadow is in its prime—and the viewing tower is not only right in scale with the planting, but also the best seat in the house.

ABOVE, TOP TO BOTTOM: *The meadow in autumn; the birdhouse was a gift to the Native Plant Garden; Carolina rose* (Rosa carolina) *has single pink flowers in summer, but grow it for the birds—they love the hips.* OPPOSITE: *The meadow as the birds view it—above the sweet gum* (Liquidambar styraciflua) *treetops.*

Plants that grow in the drier areas surrounding the wet meadow would be welcome in any flower garden.

OPPOSITE: *The NYBG gardeners call a hill near the entrance "the prairie."* Among the plants that grow there are members of the mint family (Labiatae, *typified by square stems*), including pink false dragon's teeth or obedience (Physostegia virginiana); *the buttons of faded wild bergamot* (Monarda fistulosa); *and the multitiered horsemint* (M. punctata). CLOCKWISE, FROM ABOVE: *Northern (or inland) sea oats* (Chasmanthium latifolium); *a view toward the "prairie"; and the scene from within it; sneezeweed* (Helenium autumnale); *floral wands of southern* Gaura lindheimeri; *the aromatic foliage of sweet fern* (Comptonia peregrina), *a deciduous shrub;* New York ironweed (Vernonia noveboracensis).

DIVINING INTERVENTION

Patti Goldstein was inspired by her neighbor, Kate Tyree, to transform the sodden ground behind her Long Island house into a naturalistic pond, OPPOSITE. *To stabilize the*

edge, she transplanted shrubs and perennials from adjacent thickets. A mowed path cuts through this shaggy hedgerow and leads to a bridge of her design, ABOVE, *that crosses to an island.*

"I ONCE SAW SOME OLD PIC-tures of this place," says writer Patti Goldstein about the Long Island property she shares with Sandra Powers. "There was water here—probably an inlet that connected the bays—but I guess that was before the roads were put in." However, she didn't need that confirmation to know there was water here; it was always muddy. Inspired by her neighbor, Kate Tyree (page 141), Goldstein decided to try to make a pond.

"We just dug down six inches, and it was water." The pond was dug with a backhoe, and it was done quickly, forming a quarter-acre pond fed by two natural springs. "There was a willow tree in the middle of the site, and I didn't have the heart to cut it down, so I decided to make an island to save the tree." Goldstein's West Highland terrier, Wallis, claimed the island for herself.

Herons and egrets visit fre-quently. The pond was stocked at the outset to control mosqui-toes, but now there are some fish that weren't introduced. "I guess they came as eggs on duck feet, or something." An air pump at-tached to a bubbler oxygenates the water in summer for the fish. Three merganser ducks also made the pond home. And the property, named Rabbit Run, has its share of bunnies.

The balance of nature can seem daunting. Along with the wel-come pets, there have been un-welcome pests. The muskrats are the worst. "There's a natural muskrat run back there. We can't have waterlilies—they eat them all." Still, Goldstein is unwill-ing to exterminate. "The ship-ping lanes are open. We just have to learn to live together," she says. There are a few other problems. Algae can really get going in a hot summer. Aqua-shade is a product that is like "sunglasses" for the pond. It dyes the water blue, excluding some sunlight from the depths. "It looks like Lake Como; but the color dissipates quickly." Fortifying the pond edge has also been a concern. At one place, a large naturalized plant-ing of fiddlehead ferns (*Osmunda cinnamomea*) runs down to the water. Mallows (*Hibiscus moscheu-tos*) have filled in well with their overseer's help, and most of the rest of the edge is held by what amounts to a hedgerow of Joe-pye weed, goldenrod, rhodo-dendron, phragmites, and *Rosa multiflora*.

Some problems seem to solve themselves. For a while, there was a family of Canada geese on the pond. Geese have benefited from all the development on Long Island; they used to mi-grate, but many are now year-round residents. "At first, they were so cute—just like rubber duckies in a bathtub. But then they turned into adolescent gangsters, rooting, honking, messing up the place. Then they suddenly departed. They're mo-nogamous, and I guess one of the parents must have died. Now only an occasional kid comes by for old-times' sake."

THE BLOEDEL RESERVE
BAINBRIDGE ISLAND,
WASHINGTON

"THE BLOEDEL RESERVE IT-
self should be an example of man
working harmoniously with nature; where his power to manage
is used cautiously and wisely,"
wrote Prentice Bloedel, in archi-
val material in The Bloedel Reserve collection. His vision over
several decades turned a former
family estate on Bainbridge Island, Washington, into a splen-
did sanctuary glorifying both
gardens and nature. Today, the
reserve is open by appointment,
managed by the Arbor Fund that
was set up for the purpose.

WISDOM IN THE WOODS

*Creating an attractive
environment for birds has
always been one of the goals
of the Bloedel Reserve. The
bird marsh,* RIGHT, *is a
managed wetland habitat. Red
alders (Alnus rubra or A.*

oregona), *the dominant trees,
are thinned from time to time,
and several flowering and
fruiting shrubs, such as the
white spring-blossoming
thicket serviceberry
(Amelanchier canadensis),*
ABOVE, *have been planted.*

It was appropriate—if perhaps
a bit ironic—that the estate stood
on cutover forest land, logged by
a former owner. The Bloedels
were longtime members of the
lumbering industry, too, and in
their life among the former forest
they learned a new relationship
to trees, walking the old logging
roads of the land where they had
come to live.

"We discovered that there is
grandeur in decay," wrote Bloedel about such forays into the
young mixed conifer-hardwood
stand, "the rotten logs hosting
seedlings of hemlocks, cedars,
huckleberries, the shape of a
crumbling snag. . . . Out of
these experiences came an unexpected insight," he continued.
"Respect for trees and plants re-
places indifference; one feels the
existence of a divine order. Man
is not set apart from the rest of
nature."

The reserve is by no means a
purely native landscape; formal
areas include a Japanese garden,

and a long reflection pool flanked by lawn and framed by hedges. Even more arresting than these handsome features is the moss garden—though man-made, it evokes the character of a rain forest like the greater landscape of the Pacific Northwest. Paths are safe and dry, but the visitor still feels that at any moment he or she might sink ankle-deep into the sodden carpet—warm slippers formed by stalagmites of pure jade.

Habitat for birds has long been a point of emphasis on the property. When trees were thinned, trunks were left standing up to fifteen feet to attract cavity-nesters. A university ornithologist advised designating a bird sanctuary around a pond dotted with alder islands, a carpet of ferns and sedges thriving beneath the trees. Once, it had been choked with cattails, but now it is a more balanced community with open water that birds can move through easily. Native blood currant (*Ribes sanguineum*), western azalea (*Rhododendron occidentale*), red osier dogwood (*Cornus stolonifera*), and moose-wood viburnum (*Viburnum edule*) are among the plants used to enhance the site.

OPPOSITE: *A unique double western* Trillium ovatum, *discovered in 1949, grows in redwood sorrel* (Oxalis oregana). *The Moss Garden,* TOP RIGHT, *is home to the deer fern* (Blechnum spicant). CENTER RIGHT: *The western skunk cabbage* (Lysichiton americanum) *glows among tree trunks,* CENTER LEFT AND BELOW, *where hemlocks* (Tsuga heterophylla) *are shrouded by the thick carpet.*

SANCTUARY ESTATES
FRANKLIN, WISCONSIN

FIVE YEARS OF BASELINE studies preceded the start of construction at Sanctuary Estates, a five-home housing development set beside sensitive wetlands. Today, not only is the complex of wetlands preserved, but residents live in a sixty-five-acre sanctuary for foxes, great blue herons, and other wildlife of all kinds.

The Monastery Lake area, where Sanctuary Estates is situated, includes a marsh, a tamarack swamp, and also a rare

AMONG PEACEFUL WATERS

Wetland preservation often results as a concession between developers and environmentalists. Some farsighted builders, however, recognize the aesthetic,

economic, and ecological value of these habitats. Sanctuary Estates, RIGHT, *is a development of grand houses surrounding a restored wetland in Wisconsin. Raised walks and bridges provide access between properties without disturbing the delicate ecosystem,* ABOVE.

fen where water comes from mineral-rich groundwater.

"Everyone has become a real protector of the environment," says JoAnn Gillespie, of Country Wetlands, who was called in by owner-developer Gerry Ritzo to perform studies and restoration.

White sweet clover (*Melilotus alba*), a formidable opponent, is best pulled at petal drop and the pulled plants removed from the site. But canary grass (*Phalaris arundinacea*), which forms some of the worst monotypic stands of any choking plant, has been the chief opponent. Burning has not proved effective, so a mowing program has been developed to overcome the invasion. "By timing the mowing correctly, we have been able to bring back fifteen species of plants that had been present before," says Gillespie. Spring (prior to meristem, or new plant, development) and fall mowings over a three-year period were the key. A newly developed hover-mower may prove to be an important tool.

THE NEW ENGLAND WILD
FLOWER SOCIETY—
GARDEN IN THE WOODS
FRAMINGHAM,
MASSACHUSETTS

IN 1931, WILL C. CURTIS began a garden of wild plants in Framingham, Massachusetts. Later he was joined in the effort by Howard O. Stiles, and on this naturally wooded site of very varied topography, the two built a collection of plants—wild, but not necessarily indigenous. This is not a habitat re-creation or restoration, nor does it have the synoptic or systematic assemblies of plants of a botanical garden. It is built around botanicals and its mission is to share the knowl-

THE GARDEN
IN THE WETLANDS

"Garden in the Woods" aptly describes this place's best-known feature, but the wetland plantings are equally rich. In autumn, the

Pondside, ABOVE RIGHT AND OPPOSITE, *Shady Brook,* CENTER RIGHT, *and Sunny Bog,* BELOW RIGHT, *are filled with colors from residents such as the amazing yellow pitcher plants* (Sarracenia flava), ABOVE.

edge of these plants and insight from years of growing them. In this living museum, every plant is clearly labeled with Latin and common names, country of origin, and its status if rare, threatened, or endangered.

Today, the garden is run by the New England Wild Flower Society, and members and staff are faced with a dilemma: Should the garden remain preserved as a memorial to its founders, or should all the exotic plants be removed from the forty-eight-acre grounds in the name of purity? A likely outcome is that all new plantings will be of natives, with the original gardens maintained as their creators intended.

The shady sylvan gardens for which Garden in the Woods is famed are still a major attraction, particularly when most of the ephemerals bloom in May. In recent years, the society has introduced habitat-style plantings of meadow and shaded rock gar-

den, and there is still room to grow. Among the most fascinating areas are the wet ones: the sunny bog garden, the pondside, and the shady brook.

Curtis and Stiles fashioned the original bog after wet spots in the New Jersey Pine Barrens, a generally dry plant community with very acid, often sterile soil. The uneven topography had made it possible for plants with differing moisture requirements to coexist—winterberry holly (*Ilex verticillata*) in the medium-wet areas and wild calla (*Calla palustris*) in the lowest, wettest ones, the shallow pools that

OPPOSITE: *A rivulet runs through the Sunny Bog garden— by a planting of self-hybridizing sarracenias and to a tussock sedge* (Carex stricta). ABOVE: *Winterberry* (Ilex verticillata) *has a handsome vase shape, silvery bark with age, plus berries that are the last to be eaten by the birds in winter.* ABOVE RIGHT: *A humble bridge spans Hop Brook— a managed but not meticulously maintained area.*

aquatics adore. The stars of the garden are pitcher plants (*Sarracenia* spp.) and sundews (*Drosera rotundifolia*), which grow where the water table is just below the soil surface and the nutrition-poor soil is acidic.

Other herbaceous plants include sedges (*Carex* spp.), skunk cabbage (*Lysichiton americanum*), globeflower (*Trollius laxus*), and orchids—purple fringed (*Habenaria psycodes*), white fringed (*Habenaria blephariglottis*), and grass pink (*Calopogon pulchellus*). Around these are shrubby plants including members of the heath family (*Ericaceae*) including highbush blueberry (*Vaccinium corymbosum*), sand myrtle (*Leiophyllum buxifolium*), Labrador tea (*Ledum groenlandicum*), and sheep laurel (*Kalmia angustifolia*).

The pond at Garden in the Woods was a feature from the start, but in recent years the staff has somewhat systematically filled in with more and more natives. By the waterside, *Helonias bullata,* swamp pink, originally a denizen of New Jersey swamps

where much of its habitat has been altered or destroyed, is thriving, and other natives— blue flag (*Iris versicolor*), turtle-head (*Chelone glabra*), Canada lily (*Lilium canadense*), bluestar or dogbone (*Amsonia tabernaemontana*), closed gentian (*Gentiana andrewsii*) ferns, and lobelias (both great blue, *Lobelia siphilitica,* and cardinal flower, *L. cardinalis*)—add to the show.

Near the northwest boundary of the property little has been developed, or will ever be. Here a beautiful woodland (where a stream called Hop Brook winds its way along through the brush) is managed, but not meticulously maintained. When an old pine fell, it was left in place and a path was made to run along its downed trunk. The soil here is nearly always moist, and in early spring, actually underwater. Native beeches and pines thrive on a slope beside the sodden earth and in their shadows, the two eastern clintonias bloom: speckled beadlily (*Clintonia umbellulata*) and blue beadlily (*C. borealis*).

GEORGE PURMONT AND
DAUNE PECKHAM
LITTLE COMPTON,
RHODE ISLAND

GARDEN OF FOUR PONDS

What started out as a place for recreation became much more—a wetland habitat replete with all the life that accompanies this exuberant

community. A few of the ponds have islands or peninsulas. This one, RIGHT, *is blessed with white waterlilies* (Nymphaea odorata)*. Many shrubs have found this place, such as black chokeberry* (Aronia melanocarpa)*,* ABOVE.

REMNANTS OF SOME OLD stone walls in what is now woods tell George Purmont and his wife, garden designer Daune Peckham, that the land behind their home was probably once farmed. But that was long ago, Purmont says—look at the girth of some of the second-growth trees—and probably not so successful, since the tract of land in Little Compton, Rhode Island, is too wet even to build on.

On the site, which has been in the family for more than a century, Purmont's grandfather built a pond about the size of a house many years ago. Thus began Purmont's love of water.

"My brother Wayland and I used to play in the swampy places and crawl through the tall grass," he recalls. "I can still remember the odor of blue clay."

When the boys were in their early twenties, they decided to build ponds in the wet land to make it more accessible for recreation and attractive to wildlife and so they could stock the water for fishing and to help reduce mosquitoes. The ponds were designed in place by bulldozing the scrub and small trees into windrows or berms that defined the shapes of the ponds-to-be. Then the sodden earth was scooped out, piled up on the berms, and smoothed.

The first pond was built next to the existing one and connected with a slim waterway spanned by a bridge. There are now a total of four. The property has

I LOVE TO VISIT THE WIDE-OPEN SPACES; I'M transfixed by the vision of the expansive amber prairie in autumn and the seamless sea of desert. And yet the sight that heartens me most is sheltered and snug: I love the woodland best.

Beneath the spires of the towering trees, I feel as if I have entered a cathedral built by nature for worshiping these grand totems of my faith. My fantasy home landscape would be a mixed hardwood forest with native rhododendron and rocky, fern-covered terrain traversed by a stream—not unlike the woods of North Carolina.

The forest's majesty is unmistakable, whether seen from the air in fall, ABOVE, *or from right in among the trees, such as in Muir Woods north of San Francisco,* RIGHT. *In that cathedrallike setting stand some of the planet's largest citizens, the giant redwoods (Sequoia sempervirens),* guardians of a complex forest community.*

When conditions in a woodland change, some animals never get a second foothold. Amphibians and birds are particularly vulnerable, LEFT AND ABOVE. Others such as woodchucks, RIGHT, and deer seem invincible. Electric fencing and nylon net barriers are the safest, most effective methods to keep out deer.

The woodlands of the United States—the eastern hardwood forests, the coastal conifer forests of the Northwest, the oak woodlands of central Texas and California, the pine forests of the Northeast and the Rockies—are exemplified by their enduring woody perennials, the longest-living creatures on earth. In Muir Woods, north of San Francisco, visitors can see some of the planet's largest beings, the redwoods (*Sequoia sempervirens*), in whose shade an old and complex community of plants and animals thrives, protected since around the turn of this century.

"Any fool can destroy trees," wrote John Muir, the great champion of wild spaces. "They cannot run away; and if they could, they would still be destroyed —chased and hunted down as long as fun or a dollar could be got out of [them]."

Today, Third World rain forests are falling to slash-and-burn tactics, and the United States' trees (even ones in some national forests, sold off like so many cattle to logging interests) are still dropping, though most were scraped right off the face of the emerging nation in our own eras of settlement and development. Little remains in the East, for example, and what is there, besides fragments of virgin woodland, is really new hardwood forest, regrown as the forest-turned-farmland was abandoned and young trees moved back in.

Unfortunately, the new forests are an unbalanced tangle of natives and exotics, not the same mix as the originals at all, and all too often dominated by opportunistic weedy species that don't always support the native wildlife very well.

Once the trees are cut, letting the sun in, the underlying soil quickly dries and compacts, altering— perhaps permanently—what can and will grow on the site. It can be many decades before enough leaf litter builds up from the young pioneer tree species, opportunists who jump into the cleared site, for conditions on the ground level to be right for ferns and woodland wildflowers to repopulate; some may never do so. Likewise, many animal inhabitants never get a second chance.

Recent efforts to save the habitat of the spotted owl, a native of the Northwestern woods, made its protectors the brunt of political jokes. Yet anyone who fails to recognize the pertinence of every last organism, from microbes to mankind, is in danger of sharing the owl's fate. If logging had continued, the forests the spotted owl inhabits would have been gone by the year 2000, and the owl with them.

Already in the Northwest, some trees have been felled that had been standing for more than a millennium when Christ or Buddha lived—three-thousand-plus-year-old giant sequoias, *Sequoiadendron giganteum*. These trees were America's pyramids, a true wonder of the world, and their destruction will be recalled as a memorial to the death of reason.

SAFE, SHADED HAVENS

Although I grew up in a 1950s-vintage ranch house in a typical New Jersey suburb, what I recall most vividly were the nearby places left from the pre-tract-home days—traces of a nineteenth-century Romantic landscape in which grand mansions once stood. In a vast wasteland of lawns a fifteen-foot rhododendron and mountain laurel beneath a towering hemlock formed a darkened "fort." I shared this magical playground with companions like nightcrawlers and an occasional salamander.

No wonder, then, the feelings that were stirred when I was invited into Evelyn Adams's Massachusetts garden, a hidden hollow among the trees where each spring the ground bursts forth with trillium and Virginia bluebells. Or when I was allowed to poke around in the many hidden corners of the Pennsylvania garden of Dr. Richard Lighty, where one narrow path leads to a patchwork of many distinctive forms of foamflower, *Tiarella* spp., another down into a depression bright with yellow western skunk cabbage, *Lysichiton americanum,* beside a little stream.

Trees and their understory—the kinds of places where Adams and Lighty make their gardens—are bonded to my memory. As a teenager, I traveled with my parents to the Great Smoky Mountains and saw bright orange-red carcasses of chestnut trees littering the forest floor. These trees succumbed to a devastating blight that slipped into this country in the

When an opening in the forest occurs, or when pasture land is left to revert to woods, young trees move in to fill the gap, as in this New England scene, ABOVE. *But too often the new population doesn't accurately represent the former generation and includes aliens. Good woodland management would prescribe the removal of so-called trash trees.* BELOW: *What could replace trees so precious as the giant redwoods? Just imagine if weedy eucalyptus trees were to overrun this sylvan spectacle.*

There is beauty in small things in the woodland, such as an exquisite fungus, ABOVE; the highly pleated leaves of American false hellebore (Veratrum viride), OPPOSITE; and in the velvety texture of even the tiny moss plants, RIGHT, which can be cultivated as here, in Carol Mercer's Long Island garden. Generally, moss wants a very acidic (pH 5.5), clayey, and compact soil. Scrape away any remnants of grass, rake stones and debris away, and sweep. Compress the surface by rolling or stamping on a flat board. If you live near a woodland where moss grows, just keep the spot damp for several weeks, and spores in the air will probably settle and grow. You can also transplant moss. If it is sheet moss, it will peel up in a solid mat. If it is the kind of moss that falls apart when you lift it, that's fine, too. Place the collected moss in a plastic bag to transplant as soon as possible. Scratch the surface of the prepared site with a hand fork. Place bits of the moss, green side up, around the area, about one in the center of every square foot of space. Press the moss firmly into the soil and keep it watered for a week—longer in hot weather.

wind impact on the structure by as much as half. Instead of planting in a straight line, soften the near side of the windbreak with a mixed planting of evergreen and deciduous trees, shrubs, vines, and herbaceous plants.

Trees also buffer traffic and other noise pollution; they can intercept dust with their leaves, and their roots conserve soil that might otherwise be eroded as it washes or blows away. They mediate the impact of raindrops on the soil surface, a major cause of soil compaction that too few gardeners recognize. When water (whether rain or snow) falls first onto trees, it will drip more slowly and gently onto the ground from their leaves, needles, or branches.

If you live on or purchase a property that is wooded, you might think your work is done, and I suppose that in a few places still left on earth that would be the case. But in most situations you will be facing, at best, a second-growth woodland in need of rehabilitation, a place of Japanese bittersweet and honeysuckle perhaps, or numerous seedlings and saplings of trash tree species. A chain saw, as well as several handsaws and pruners and a pole saw/pruner, will be essential to almost everyone who sets out to garden a woodland habitat, but these tools must be used with caution and common sense. Never remove a tree without a lot of thought—even dead trees have value as shelter for such prehistoric treasures as pileated woodpeckers. Remember the sentiments of the poet William Blake: A tree is an object that moves some to tears, to others it is only a green thing that stands in the way. Gardeners should find themselves in the former category.

When Sara Stein came to her New York property,

already profiled in the grasslands section, she couldn't even get through the woods. The understory was choked by catbrier and poison ivy; many of the trees were weedy species. She has spent years clearing the undesirables from the underbrush, but just as soon as she finished the last area she had to start over again, where the aggressors were already getting a renewed foothold. Planting acceptable species on the woodland floor helped discourage them, but a regular ongoing maintenance program will continue to be necessary. Gardening in the woods is a commitment to woodlands management.

Do not go overboard. Clearing all the brush from beneath the trees indiscriminantly might cause the ultimate destruction of the community, eliminating conditions that foster welcome seedlings and even the older trees. Do not rake out the litter on the forest floor, either; it is nature's compost. Forests collect their debris and break it down slowly. For example, soils in conifer forests, in particular, are acid to very acid and therefore nutrient-deficient. The soil life is limited by the acidity, and as a result litter can remain a decade or more before decomposition is complete.

A WOODLAND INVENTORY

Before setting out armed with tools, it is wise to catalog all existing trees. Using a comprehensive field guide, key out and list or map all the trees. Note the natives, and also which plants are not just American but local—those that are indigenous to your area. You might even consider a system of tagging the trees with ribbons color-coded by species, or simply by which ones stay and which ones go.

The goal is not so much to tally the natives as to rogue out the weed species, trees whose propensity to seed or otherwise spread themselves around makes them gluttons of the landscape. In the mid-Atlantic states, that might be *Ailanthus altissima,* the tree of heaven, brought to the United States in the eighteenth century in an ill-fated attempt to establish a silk industry here. Silkworms turned up their noses at ailanthus leaves, but the tree loved America, and

The trees of New England, ABOVE LEFT, *just before the leaves drop to replenish the dark and moist forest floor,* OPPOSITE, *where life in the woodland begins and ends. Other trees, such as the weeping Brewer spruce* (Picea brewerana), ABOVE, *from the Siskiyou Mountains of Oregon, leave the crunchy sound of needles underfoot.*

think of the area as your very own nursery source. List worthy ones to be saved from the bulldozer for relocating elsewhere in the landscape.

When you have completed this thorough inventory, begin to remove weed trees, shrubs, and vines, according to the best methods for each species. Those that will resprout from their roots cannot simply be cut down; again, the local extension service or botanical garden may be able to suggest the least-toxic method of eliminating such plants.

Always evaluate the amount of damage that uprooting a tree will do to its neighbors—not just whether its trunk will strike another on the way down, but whether its extraction will damage the roots of other desired plants. Some people take trees out gradually over several years, cutting them to about two feet the first year. If the plant doesn't sprout a year later, you might then choose to leave the stump for good, and even incorporate it into a permanent bench or table design. If it does resprout, rub off the new growth a few times and see if it

finally succumbs. If not, it will have to go by pulling, burning, or some other method—stick to those that are environmentally safe.

If you own or purchase a wooded site on which you plan to build, you may have to do your inventory quickly, before a single piece of equipment rolls onto the land and over tree roots. Identify the trees you want to save, then make this a priority by writing it into the construction contract.

The hazards to trees from building (or paving, or excavating for a drywell or cesspool, or even from parking a car on their unseen underground root zones) cannot be overstated. Besides the obvious damage from impact with heavy machinery (including the family car!) soil compaction kills trees. Have your contractor erect a sturdy fence around each tree

Many trees enjoy the company of their kin, such as ponderosa pine (Pinus ponderosa) *from the Rocky Mountains,* ABOVE. *Some redwood trees grow vegetatively from the burls that surround the base of old trees. Now these giant sequoia,* ABOVE LEFT, *form a circle around the spot where their long-gone parent stood.*

to be saved, not right up against the trunk but as far out as the dripline, an imaginary line corresponding to the circumference of the branches. Plan to supervise the process, since damage may not be visible until a tree dies a year or two later.

The effect on trees from chemicals used during construction, like pH-altering concrete and paints, is significant. Piling up soil over a tree's roots, or against its trunk, during grading work is also inviting disaster. A mere six inches more or less of soil can have catastrophic consequences.

If the grade must be changed near a tree, bring in a tree surgeon or landscaping professional with expertise on protecting trees during construction. Landscape architect Ron Lutsko of San Francisco was brought into a project because some California live

Fallen pine needles, ABOVE, form a wonderful mulch. Their coarse texture and low moisture, combined with a high acid content, allow them to last for years: It can take ten years for them to decompose. ABOVE RIGHT: The perfect place to rest and relax may already exist in a wooded spot, such as this one at Tower Hill.

oaks were dying more than a year after construction was complete on the client's new home. He discovered that as much as six feet of rubble and soil had been moved onto the trees' root zones, cutting off oxygen and water, and began excavating to try to save them. He built retaining walls around their bases, then filled the outside space with gravel to allow for good drainage where the accumulation couldn't be removed—and most of the trees survived.

Just as trees do not want to grow half submerged in rubble, they would not volunteer to a life as soldiers, all lined up single file. Look at natural places where trees grow, or at paintings and historic photographs of the ancient forests before they were cut. They hardly resemble rigid plantings on graph paper. Leave such orderly layouts to the tree farms.

"Trees are much like human beings and enjoy each other's company," wrote Jens Jensen, ". . . with their branches interlaced they give an expression of friendship."

MIXED FRUIT

When planning a biohedge, or any other use of berried shrubs and trees in the natural habitat garden, consider the birds' needs carefully. Summertime food and wintertime food requirements may be very different; the fruit that suits one bird in summer may not be its wintertime choice at all.

High-lipid fruits (those that include fats) like spicebush (*Lindera benzoin*) and sassafras (*Sassafras albidum*) are ideal for the premigratory phase since they are intensely calorie-rich, perfect for storing up reserves for birds' incredible long-distance journeys. In spring and summer, high-sugar fruits like blackberry, elderberry, raspberry, and cherries are more to birds' liking. And wintertime food in cold-winter areas must be high in carbohydrates. Winterberry (*Ilex verticillata*), poison ivy (*Toxicodendron radicans*), and sumac (*Rhus* spp.) are ideal for meeting these needs. Too many gardeners wishing to welcome wildlife focus only on birds' wintertime feeding requirements. Refer to birding books, or contact your local Audubon Society chapter or the National Wildlife Federation for further help in designing a locally appropriate, year-round avian food supply.

LEFT, TOP TO BOTTOM:
Nuts from California buckeye (Aesculus californica); *red prickly pears; yellow fruits of* Ferocactus *spp.; tiny red berries of the* Ceanothus *cultivar 'Dark Star'.*

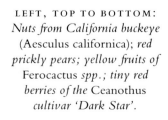

WOODLAND TIPS

Plan for a smooth transition to your woods, both for aesthetic reasons and wildlife benefits. Develop the intermediate level between lawn or low-growing herbaceous plants and trees with smaller trees and shrubs.

Creating paths, rather than allowing random movement through the wooded area, may prove beneficial in rekindling the plants of the floor, like sedges, ferns, wildflowers, and mosses.

If the soil needs improvement, try to stick to amendments that are as close to the natural forest elements as possible: leaf mold, for example, particularly from trees similar to those in the planting, should be used instead of peat moss or some other foreign substance.

Spacing is critical when planting trees, and to only a slightly lesser degree shrubs. These are long-term additions to the landscape. Plan for their eventual size, and space accordingly.

Cutting back and pruning woody plants yields woodchips, which should be composted before they are used in the landscape. Uncomposted chips rob nutrition from the underlying soil. When mulching with composted chips, use a thin layer, and never pile them up against tree trunks.

Don't haul away all the debris; fallen trunks are beautiful, and invite diversity in the form of fungi, mosses, lichens, and their companion insects into the woodland.

Use some of the brush from the clearing of the woods to create a brush pile, a favorite haunt for birds and other animals.

Where there is a soil-compaction problem, which can mean death to trees, the best antidote is a mulch of leaves. An appropriate organic mulch encourages an abundance of soil-aerating lifeforms beneath the surface.

Where trees will remain in a lawn area, remove the sod from underneath them, all the way out to the dripline. Replace it with a thin layer of appropriate mulch (leaf mold, pine needles, composted chips), or a ground cover.

Never flush-cut a tree when pruning; flush cuts injure trunk tissue, which can be devastating to the tree's health. Do not leave long stubs that encourage disease, either. Never damage the branch collar, in most species a raised ring that differentiates trunk from branch.

Never paint a pruning cut or a wound to a tree; let the tree heal itself.

Transplanting can be a money-saving strategy, and many seedlings, in particular, are easily moved. While still in leaf, mark the trees to be moved, and prepare the holes. Then, when the leaves fall (November in many areas), transplant the tree.

When tree roots are damaged from construction or transplanting, be sure to recut them cleanly with a pruner before replanting. Crushed or shredded roots don't take up moisture effectively.

Some tree work, especially on older specimens, is not for the gardener to do, but for a professional. Hire a licensed, insured arborist who demonstrates a strong knowledge of native trees.

OPPOSITE, TOP TO BOTTOM: *False Solomon's-seal* (Smilacina racemosa); *lowbush blueberry* (Vaccinium angustifolium); *gray dogwood* (Cornus racemosa); *American highbush cranberry* (Viburnum trilobum). COUNTERCLOCKWISE FROM TOP: *Berries are as ornamental as they are edible, but some, such as poison ivy and baneberry, are toxic to humans. Baneberry* (Actaea rubra) *and doll's-eyes* (A. pachypoda) *in Judith Stark's wildlife garden; doll's-eyes (detail); fragrant thimbleberry* (Rubus odoratus); *sugarbush* (Rhus ovata) *is a frost-tender cousin of the sumacs.*

AMERICA'S OWN RHODODENDRONS

In much of America, rhododendrons and azaleas have become synonymous with spring and are a mainstay of nearly every home landscape. Unfortunately, the majority of home owners have overlooked the native American rhododendrons, many of which are beginning to be promoted in nurseries.

Most of our native rhododendrons come from the Southeast and the Pacific Northwest, where soil and climate conditions are ideal for them. Because rhododendrons are acid-loving plants, they are not appropriate for many central areas of the nation, where alkaline soil is common.

Among the North American species are many evergreens, including *Rhododendron chapmanii,* which grows in the Florida sand dunes in conditions that could not be more unlikely for a member of this genus. At the top of the continent, *R. lapponicum* thrives in the Arctic tundra near the pole and down to the northernmost forests.

The Southeast is practically synonymous with the genus. It is the home of the twenty- to thirty-five-foot *R. maximum,* the rosebay rhododendron, a familiar evergreen of the Great Smoky Mountains that blooms early to midsummer, and whose range extends into Massachusetts and up to Maine. In Newport, Rhode Island, for example, the mansions are sheltered from the street by giant specimen rosebays.

From the Carolinas come *R. minus* and the very similar *R. carolinianum,* with flowers in white or shades of pink in late spring. There are many cultivated varieties, including one with blotches of yellow on the white flowers and narrow leaves (*R. minus* 'Album'). One of the sturdiest of all the southeastern rhododendrons and parent to many hardy hybrids is *R. catawbiense,* another Smoky Mountain native. Large, mounded shrubs cover the rolling terrain of central to western North Carolina in June with drifts of lilac-purple to pink, and sometimes white, at elevations as high as six thousand feet.

About the hardiest native rhododendron is *R. vaseyi,* the pinkshell azalea, and it is also very showy, blooming pink or sometimes white before the leaves emerge. It also offers red fall foliage.

In the Northwest, *R. macrophyllum* is the Catawba's western counterpart. This species, which grows along the coast, blooms in late spring and has voluptuous, bell-shaped flowers of rose-purple with brown spots. *R. albiflorum* grows in the mountains of the Northwest and into Colorado, but hasn't found its way into many gardens yet.

Rhododendron occidentale, the western azalea, is a deciduous species appreciated by sophisticated English gardeners for over a century. It is most valued there for the role it played in the development of numerous prized hybrids—many of which came back to adorn American gardens in the West. It is a medium-sized shrub with leaves and flowers coming at the same time; the flowers are creamy white to pale pink and

pale to chrome yellow at the base. The leaves turn yellow to orange to ruby in fall.

There are more than a dozen deciduous azalea-type rhododendron species native to Georgia alone.

The deep coral flowers of *R. prunifolium,* the plum-leaf azalea, are produced from August to September in my garden, earlier in its native territory. But it is the early spring species, particularly the fragrant ones, that are more popular.

The sweet azalea (*R. canescens*) is the first to bloom in March to April in Georgia, along with another fragrant species, the yellow-flowered *R. austrium.* In mid-April, *R. flammeum* (syn. *R. speciosum*) produces its yellow, salmon, or pink blossoms; from the lowlands of Georgia and South Carolina, it is not as hardy as some and is not fragrant.

Rhododendron periclymenoides (syn. *R. nudiflorum*), the pinxterbloom or honeysuckle azalea, is better known as a parent of the popular Ghent hybrids. It is floriferous (April), producing pale pink blooms with a red tube that are honey-and-spice scented, and survives with minimal care in an extensive range of hardiness up through Massachusetts.

Rhododendron prinophyllum (syn. *R. roseum*), rose-shell azalea, a very hardy species that ranges to Quebec, offers its pink, intensely clove-scented flowers from April to May in Georgia. *R. albamense,* Alabama azalea, is a fragrant white species blooming around the same time. *R. atlanticum* hails from along the Atlantic coastal plain; it is a small, stoloniferous shrub whose bluish green foliage is a fine contrast to the fragrant white to pinkish blooms.

One of the most brilliant Georgians is *R. calendulaceum,* the flame azalea, whose flowers (May and June) range from yellow to orange to scarlet. It also has fine fall color, making it one of the nation's showiest all-around rhododendron species. About two weeks later than *R. calendulaceum,* look for the outstanding red or orange-red blooms of *R. bakeri,* the Cumberland azalea, which is less heat tolerant than its close relative.

The swamp azalea, *R. viscosum,* grows by freshwater ponds in Cape Cod and down to the Alabama swamps—a star for wet-soil areas. Its clove-scented flowers are white to light pink, May to June.

Some southern individuals of *R. arborescens,* the sweet azalea, bloom late—July, and perhaps even August—though others bloom in early summer. The range of this plant is wide, from Georgia up into Pennsylvania and New York. The fragrant, white funnel-form flowers are set off by a reddish style (the elongated part of the pistil). *R. serrulatum* is about the last to bloom, often into September, its fragrant, white flowers sometimes blushed pink.

Some of our native rhododendrons include: ABOVE, LEFT TO RIGHT, *pinxterbloom* (Rhododendron periclymenoides *syn.* R. nudifloram); *the mid- to late-summer-flowering plum-leaved rhododendron* (Rhododendron prunifolium); Catawba *rhododendron* (R. catawbiense); *western azalea* (R. occidentale), *prized for its fall color; pink-shell azalea* (R. vaseyi).

DICK AND SALLY LIGHTY
KENNETT SQUARE,
PENNSYLVANIA

WHY THERE IS NOT AN AMERI-can plant bearing the specific epithet *lightii* or at least one called 'Lighty's Gem' or some such thing is hard to understand, for Dick Lighty is a champion of our native flora.

Dr. Richard Lighty has been at the native game since at least the day in 1958 when as a young plant geneticist, he collected a solitary trillium plant from the woods of the Pocono Mountains and carried it home. Today, more than fifteen hundred stems from that *Trillium grandiflorum*

TWO WORLDS, ONE GARDEN

fill the garden that he and his wife, Sally, have built over thirty-plus years near the Delaware border in Pennsylvania.

Trilliums are notoriously slow to multiply, and have therefore been shunned by the nursery industry as noncommercial. But this variety, which Lighty has recently named 'Quicksilver', reproduces three or four times faster than other clones. Lighty has begun to distribute 'Quicksilver' to native-plant nurseries so that the consumer can have ethically propagated trilliums at a reasonable price for the garden.

The story of the trillium and of Lighty's career are one: a commitment to bringing better selections of native plants to our gardens. The former administrator of the Longwood Graduate Program at the University of Delaware, Lighty has been the director of Mt. Cuba Center for the Study of Piedmont Flora since 1983.

Even such a dedicated native-

There's an arresting planting in the Lighty garden, BELOW. *It's a circle of native Allegheny spurge* (Pachysandra procumbens),

framed by a wreath of Asian Pachysandra terminalis *'Variegata'. East meets West here—except over the bridge in the all-native garden where,* RIGHT, *spectacular wildflowers can be found, such as yellow lady's slipper orchid* (Cypripedium calceolus).

plant type as Lighty suffers from a bit of horticultural schizophrenia. The symbols of his split passion are evident at Springwood, the undulating seven-and-a-half-acre property he and his wife so aptly named, for it is a woodland rich and moist with the presence of underground springs.

Plants of Asia share the stage with Americans—a wave of variegated Asian *Pachysandra terminalis* with a dollop of native American *Pachysandra procumbens* in its midst about sums things up. As if to find a way to manage his dual botanical enthusiasm, Lighty built a little footbridge over a stream that crosses the place, officially marking one bank as the international side and the other Americans-only.

On the native side, a frothy crazy quilt of foamflowers, each displaying a different leaf shape or surface pattern, coaxes visitors down a path. Around a corner, a clump of golden *Deschampia flexuosa* 'Aurea' positively glows a luminescent chartreuse in a shaft of light.

A favorite feature is the Lightys' "symbolic meadow," a kind of king-sized perennial garden made up of herbaceous giants

In some ways this appears to be a conventional landscape, LEFT, *but the Continental contrast can be seen again,* ABOVE LEFT, *where American pachysandra is separated by an ocean of lawn from its Asian mate.* OPPOSITE, CLOCKWISE FROM NEAR RIGHT: *Phlox and trillium; woodland natives; a selection of foamflower* (Tiarella cordifolia) *isolated for leaf shape and markings;* Deschampsia flexuosa *'Aurea';* Cornus sericea *'Silver and Gold'.*

typical of meadows and grass-lands. In the grass-dominated mix, color is not the guiding element, though *Eupatorium fistulosum,* liatris, *Vernonia altissima,* cassia, and coreopsis are represented. Texture and form are all-important here, a revealing lesson in design.

A walk in the Lightys' garden is like that: bits of botany and horticulture gently interspersed throughout the beauty. A tip on how to divide a trillium might be offered ("Right after bloom when foliage is hard, and they will suffer no setback," he says), or propagating that luscious native pachysandra said to be so difficult ("In early July, grab hold of the new shoots when they are reasonably hard and jerk them out, then plant as you would rooted cuttings").

Several decades of life with deer has yielded lessons, too. A seven-foot fence of plastic netting hung between the trees has finally given way to barriers of chicken wire and a heavier cable.

Soil preparation is a well-oiled routine at Springwood, where the Lightys smother a new area to be planted with ten inches of woodchips, and then use a glyphosate herbicide to knock down anything that dares to push through. "The chips mean fewer chemicals are needed to kill existing vegetation; they enrich the soil; and they act as mulch until the desirables fill in," he says.

Not all the plants get names, and some will never be seen beyond the Lighty garden. A lipstick-pink selection of the trillium, for instance, will probably never make the catalog headlines, as pretty as it is.

"I would have to call that one 'Molasses'," Lighty says with a laugh, "because it's slow as molasses in January to propagate."

One planting dominates the landscape, LEFT, *in the sunny open area beyond the swimming pool. It is the "symbolic meadow"—a perennial bed occupied by the behemoths of the meadows and prairies, including Joe-pye weed and tall ironweed* (Vernonia altissima), *which shoots up through lower plants in late summer, along with some cultivated ornamental grass varieties.* ABOVE LEFT: *Wild senna, or cassia* (Cassia marilandica), *flowers on one side of the Joe-pye weed; northern sea oats bears its animated chevron-shaped spikelets on the other,* ABOVE.

IT HAS BEEN THIRTY YEARS since Pamela Copeland set about to bring the wildings closer to home. The surrounding woods on her Delaware Valley estate, Mt. Cuba, were rich with colonies of wildflowers, but closer to the house, extensive formal gardens dominated the scene.

The large naturalistic garden she added in the early 1960s made a perfect counterpoint to the formality, and also something more: a landscape that could silence even the harshest

BUILDING BETTER NATIVES

critic, the kind who dismisses native-plant gardening as either too wild-looking or too limited in its choice of plants.

It did not take long for Copeland to learn where native plants came from: namely, that they are plucked unscrupulously from the wild to be offered up for sale. In that sad realization, a conservationist was born.

Today, the Mt. Cuba Center for the Study of Piedmont Flora is a living native-plant guidebook, revealing a select portion of America's great natural diversity. Whole glades of flowering native shrubs—rhododendron, fothergilla, and kalmia among them—are underplanted with a tapestry of wildflowers. Phlox, foamflower, dicentras, and ferns are planted in sheets. Here and there along the broad, mulched paths are some less-familiar faces, like a native astilbe (*Astilbe biternata*), taller than the typical Asian garden varieties with stately cream-colored plumes, or

The woodland path at Mt. Cuba Center is in its prime in mid-spring, RIGHT. *Under a spreading American dogwood (Cornus florida), herbaceous*

perennial natives bloom, such as blue wild sweet William (Phlox divaricata), columbine (Aquilegia canadensis), and a tiny white-flowered native sedum, wild stonecrop (Sedum ternatum). A wooden bench makes a place to sit among the wildflowers, ABOVE.

PORTOLA VALLEY RANCH
PORTOLA VALLEY,
CALIFORNIA

A CENTURY OF OVERGRAZ-
ing had thwarted the emerging
oak seedlings on the land that
was to become Portola Valley
Ranch, a progressive residential
community and nature preserve
in the foothills of the Santa Cruz
Mountains, about thirty miles
south of San Francisco.

It was the oaks—young and
old representatives of six species
of the genus *Quercus*—around
which the plan for building on
the rolling site was formed after
developer Joseph Whelan purchased the 450 acres of coastal

ACORNS TO OAKS

oak woodland in 1974. It was
on these acres that he created
an early foray into controlled-
use development. The landscape
architect Nancy Hardesty was
brought in to create a strategy for
accomplishing this, and that
would also protect wildlife habitats of more than 125 resident animal species, stabilize the soil,
and recharge existing water-
sheds. About 200 homes were to
be clustered on 76 of the 450
acres so that the whopping share
would remain open, traversed
with nature trails. Although the
oaks are the main focus, chaparral, grassland, mixed evergreen
forest, and other habitat communities also exist on-site.

The oak woodland environ-
mental ethic Hardesty devised
protected existing trees (each one
was numbered, evaluated, and
given the care required) and renewed the oak forest, which includes coastal live oak (*Quercus
agrifolia*), canyon or golden oak

(*Q. chrysolepis*), blue oak (*Q.
douglasii*), California black oak
(*Q. kelloggii*), and valley or California white oak (*Q. lobata*). Heritage trees, some of them gnarled
and four hundred years old, are
treated as esteemed members of
the community. Home owners,
as well as their children, have
been educated in the protection
and regeneration of the oaks, including how to plant and nurture
acorns into young trees.

Hardesty wrote a newsletter
called "Nature Notes," which
was distributed periodically to
home owners to teach them to
care for the environment's other
inhabitants, both plants and animals, offering guidelines on
everything from local plant communities for help in choosing
landscape plants to wise watering
practices and feeding of birds.

Even the views are safe here.
With houses nestled below the
ridgelines of the hills and even
open-sided carports built instead
of traditional garages, the award-
winning community is meant to
stay as is, or better.

*In the mid-1970s, a pioneer
experiment in controlled-use
development was begun in the
coastal hills south of San
Francisco. Every effort was made
to cause the least disturbance and
even to restore the grassland,*

*chaparral, and oak woodland while
constructing two hundred homes.
The benefit has been exquisite
settings with native plants, RIGHT,
and spectacular uninterrupted
views, OPPOSITE. But the
landscape still functions "normally."
People who wanted lawn have
native-grass plantings, ABOVE.*

EVELYN
(MRS. ERNEST) ADAMS
WELLESLEY HILLS,
MASSACHUSETTS

THE SECRET GARDEN

*The path through Evelyn
Adams's garden forms a circle
around a solid blanket
of plants dominated by
wake-robin* (Trillium
grandiflorum) *and Virginia
bluebells* (Mertensia
virginica), RIGHT.
However, many other trillium

*species and North American
ephemerals live there, too.*
ABOVE: *"The thinking
stone" was christened years
ago when Adams's husband
came out to the garden to find
a little boy sitting on the large
rock. When asked what he
was doing there, the boy
replied, "Thinking."*

MANY DECADES OF FOOT-
steps have worn smooth the narrow pathways through Evelyn
Adams's hidden little garden, a
naturally secluded corner of the
property with an errant tree
branch "gate" that must be lifted
to gain access.

Adams, a native Vermonter,
began making the garden in
Wellesley Hills, Massachusetts,
nearly fifty years ago, beginning
with four trilliums passed along
to her from family land, along
with some daffodils. As her interest in the daffodils waned, her

love of the trilliums grew, and
she has divided them faithfully
every spring since, just after they
stop blooming, and also gathers
and scatters their seed to help the
incredible colony grow. In it are
represented more than half a
dozen of the thirty or so American species including literally
thousands of individual plants.

Also from Vermont, from the
basement of her husband's
grandfather's home, came a
large, rectangular rock that the
Adamses set into the garden as a
feature. One morning, Evelyn's
husband went out and found a
young boy sitting upon it.

"What are you doing?" he
asked the boy.

"I'm thinking," the child replied, and ever since it has been
called the thinking stone.

The native canopy of dog-
wood (*Cornus florida*) is under
stress from *discula,* the anthrac-
nose-type fungus threatening
this cherished native tree, but a

THE NEW YORK
BOTANICAL GARDEN
FOREST
BRONX, NEW YORK

IT STANDS IN DEFIANCE OF all around it, as if the last several centuries—from the arrival of the first Old World explorer on the Hudson River to the enduring age of high-rises—had not even happened.

The New York Botanical Garden Forest, 40 acres at the heart of a 250-acre, century-old institution, has managed to hang on as the largest remnant of the forest that once covered much of the metropolitan area. It has never been cut, neither for agriculture

A GENTLE HELPING HAND

When people hear that there is a forty-acre untouched woodland in New York City, they are incredulous. But it's true. Within the 250-acre, 100-year-old New York Botanical Garden is a

managed, but not maintained, forest; the glittering attraction is the Bronx River, RIGHT. *Foliage color comes from maples, oaks, tulip trees, sycamore, and sweet gum. Glacier-deposited rocks are features as well,* ABOVE.

nor for development. Some trees within the rugged, hilly tract of mixed hardwoods and hemlock are as old as three hundred years, living on despite air pollution, trampling by many millions of feet—and the pocketknives determined to leave their messages in the bark.

This forty acres is not a garden, the staff members who manage it are quick to point out. It is a living organism, protected and examined by them in extensive studies of the forest ecology. Their basically hands-off policy means that here, disease, damage, and even death are recorded but almost nothing is removed— snags (dead standing trees) are left as insect food and animal shelters, for instance. Even the great old hemlocks (*Tsuga canadensis*), besieged by the potentially deadly pest, the woolly adelgid, that is devastating the region's hemlocks, are monitored but not treated.

The native canopy of towering tulip trees (*Liriodendron tulipifera*),

birch (*Betula* spp.), sweetgum (*Liquidambar styraciflua*), cherry (*Prunus* spp.), oaks (*Quercus* spp.), and hemlock provide cover for increasingly large natural stands of trout lily (*Erythronium americanum*), mayapple (*Podophyllum peltatum*), and other ephemerals. But until a path system was established (mulched with woodchips to fit into the forest as well as possible) to limit visitor impact on the greater area, ground-level vegetation was having a hard time. Now, stress to the floor has been greatly reduced and the wildflowers, sedges (*Carex* spp.), and even grasses like little bluestem (*Andropogon scoparius* or *Schizachyrium scoparium*), in areas that get relatively high light, are rebounding nicely.

Besides stabilizing the floor, a prime objective of woodland management is to get the native canopy reestablished. Opportunists like Amur cork tree (*Phellodendron amurense*), a Chinese species, and Norway maple (*Acer platanoides*) have seeded themselves into the mix and shut out native seedlings.

Though the overall policy is one of nonintervention, some removals of trash tree species like these are performed, but carefully. Weighed into the decision of whether to remove even a modest-sized tree is the degree of disturbance it will cause. When the additional light reaches the forest floor, what will its effect be? All too often, says Ed Roy, manager of the Forest Project, such light increase favors the exotic species of the forest floor.

"You have to be really careful,

case by case, to understand the impact," he explains. In some cases, it's architecturally impossible to get the tree out without damaging the root system of another.

"And in other cases," says Roy, "the tree is performing a function that needs to be addressed." Introducing small native trees and shrubs to shade the ground where the tree was removed can mediate the impact.

The signs that this kind of management works abound on the forest floor: the little bluestem and increased population of seedlings are encouraging.

"Our job is a difficult one," says Roy, "to use management practices that enhance native species over nonnatives." The fact that this undertaking occurs in a small pocket tucked into one of the most populated urban centers on earth should steel the habitat gardener. Preserving and protecting one tree or a small woodlot should seem a little less daunting.

The river flows to a series of falls, which are popular attractions, RIGHT. *Some of the best views of the falling water,* ABOVE, *are afforded from elegant bridges.*

WING HAVEN, FORMER
GARDEN OF EDWIN AND
ELIZABETH CLARKSON
CHARLOTTE, NORTH
CAROLINA

ELIZABETH CLARKSON WAS A habitat gardener from the beginning, although when she began her formal garden in the 1920s, on bare red clay scraped clean for farming, that horticultural concept did not exist. It would be more than half a century before the native-plant movement really arrived, but by then Clarkson and her husband, Edwin, had hosted uncountable numbers of birds on the three acres they called Wing Haven. More than

PLOT FOR THE BIRDS

Habitat-style gardens are not necessarily new or informal. Wing Haven is devoted to birds. Nearly all the plants have been selected to provide shelter or food. Mahonia flower buds, BELOW, *will*

eventually produce berries that are favorites of cedar waxwings. RIGHT, TOP TO BOTTOM: *A mirror set into a brick arch is covered with netting to keep the birds from flying into the glass. The view from the bench across the garden's formal axis. Wood-duck boxes hang from trees. Carolina snailseed (Cocculus carolinus).* OPPOSITE: *The path continues to wilder parts of the garden.*

140 distinct species were recorded in the Clarkson years.

Wing Haven, now a public garden in the quiet Charlotte neighborhood where the Clarksons lived until 1988, was not just ahead of its time. It is proof positive that a structured design can be a thriving habitat.

Despite the extensive system of symmetrical brick paths, boxwood parterres, and other traditional elements, wild is the overriding word at Wing Haven. Muscadine grapes, mulberries, wild cherries, and privet (today, *Viburnum rufidulum* [rusty blackhaw] or *Vaccinium arboreum* [farkleberry] could be substituted for that exotic) grow together in a delectable jumble. Elsewhere, wild grape, trumpet vine (*Campsis radicans*) and greenbrier (*Smilax rotundifolia*) tangle their way over dogwoods and cherries. Holly, elderberry, pokeweed, mahonia, viburnum, and eleagnus (again, one to avoid because of its propensity to self-sow) contribute to the picture, too.

The place is like a living fruit salad served up in thicket form, precisely geared to avian tastes.

The Clarksons catered to their birds, not just with seed-filled feeders, but with natural features chosen to give them both food and shelter: berried plants at every turn, snags (dead trees) left standing, fallen trunks left to decay in place, piled-up brush for a safe hiding place, just enough thorns to deter predators, numerous small pools—and dripping faucets everywhere, for nothing fascinates, or satisfies, a bird more. The Clarksons first erected a wood duck box in the 1950s, and mating pairs have fledged young nearly every year.

Elizabeth's greatest vision may have been her stand against chemicals. She knew better, and so her birds survived. In the 1940s and 1950s, during municipal DDT-spray programs to reduce insects, Elizabeth went out in her nightgown in the predawn hours and stood in the road to stop the trucks from spraying her block, a proper southern housewife's brand of passive resistance. Her cul-de-sac was eventually taken off the spray route.

Indeed, Wing Haven grew wild, perhaps to a fault. Elizabeth Clarkson didn't even like to pull volunteer seedlings since her darling birds had planted them. As nature would have it, the thinning took place anyway, if belatedly and anything but gradually: In 1989, Hurricane Hugo devastated the region, taking down more than seventy-five trees on the Clarksons' small property alone. And so the habitat continues to evolve.

SAM AND BEV RYBURN
DOVER, MASSACHUSETTS

WHEN SAM AND BEV RYBURN
first saw the site of their future
home some thirty years ago,
they were smitten—although
friends, family, and even the
real-estate broker warned that
they were in for trouble with
such a "difficult" piece of land.
But it was the imposing rock
outcropping and the many large
boulders that attracted them to
the suburban Boston property.

To the Ryburns, then novice
gardeners who had been living in
the congestion of New York
City, this wooded land seemed

BUILT ON SOLID ROCK

*Few set out to make a
museum garden, but the
Ryburns have created a place
where native plants are
thoughtfully displayed and
accurately labeled. This
garden lies across a bridge,*

ABOVE RIGHT, *in a hollow
below the house and is home
to blue dogbane* (Amsonia
tabernaemontana), ABOVE,
and trillium, CENTER
RIGHT. *A stream trickles
through the garden,* RIGHT,
and into constructed pools.
OPPOSITE: *Blue phlox bask
beneath thousands of dogwood
bracts that hover like
butterflies.*

like paradise. It turned out that
there were reasons why the spot
had never been developed; what
finally became the Ryburns' land
had served as the local rock de-
pository for farmers clearing
their own acres. However, even
in the early days, before the couple began gardening, the property had more than thirty
wildflower species growing in
the moist, thin soil.

The Ryburns' initial goal was
to make a beautiful wildflower
garden, but soon it became
building a showcase—a mu-
seum, perhaps—of the wild
woodland flora of their region.
The basin-shaped garden in the
hollow below the house today
contains winding gravel pathways that take the visitor to
within inches of nearly every
plant, all clearly labeled with tags
that rival any botanical garden's.

Twenty years after the Ryburns started, 270-plus herbaceous species of plants coexist on

the same "difficult" site, including remarkable stands of pink lady's slipper (*Cypripedium acaule*)—plants the Ryburns didn't purchase (and couldn't, since even today it defies propagators) but simply encouraged so that existing colonies now produce up to 175 flowers at a time. Unfortunately, unless like the Ryburns you "inherit" such treasures, they must be admired in botanical gardens and the wild for now. Instead, start with easier ones such as *C. calceolus pubescens,* the yellow lady's slipper, which is slowly becoming available in number from ethical commercial sources. Or start as the Ryburns did by purchasing a single plant at a wildflower society sale and exercising the key trait of the wildflower gardener: the virtue of patience. Today, their once-solitary plant has grown to bear sixty-five flowers.

The garden is also home to enormous stands of single and double bloodroot (*Sanguinaria canadensis* and *S. c. multiplex,* or 'Flore Pleno'), mayapple (*Podophyllum peltatum*), and wild ginger (*Asarum canadense*). Seven trillium species, violets, and phloxes add to the spring color.

Close to the house, Sam, a for- mer chemical engineer who in his retirement gardens full time, has made a more formal rock garden representing the flora of many lands. A path leads up through the giant outcropping to a flat pad covered with the tiny native bluets (*Houstonia caerulea*) and down the other side, across a bridge over a series of pools. The water moving from one pool to another draws a wide variety of birds. This is the Ryburns' collector's area, where exotics such as Japanese jack-in-the-pulpit are contained in a carefully managed space, peacefully commingling with their native cousins.

OPPOSITE, ABOVE FAR LEFT: Viola labradorica *climbs some rock below* Iris cristata *foliage.* NEAR LEFT: *Rock doesn't thwart interrupted fern (*Osmunda claytoniana) *to the left of a dwarf hemlock.* OPPOSITE, BELOW: *The rare pink lady's slipper* (Cypripedium acaule) *should not be purchased or transplanted.* ABOVE, CLOCKWISE FROM LEFT: *Three flowers repeat trillium's leitmotif; a mature colony of bloodroot (*Sanguinaria canadensis); *an eternal sign of spring: cinnamon fern crosiers; the venerable yellow lady's slipper orchids.*

THE ARTHUR L. MENZIES
MEMORIAL GARDEN OF
NATIVE PLANTS
SAN FRANCISCO,
CALIFORNIA

EPILOGUE

Quaking aspen (Populus tremuloides), OPPOSITE, *provide patterned gray bark for winter interest after silver-dollar leaves turn yellow and drop. But the spring sea of meadow foam (Limnanthes*

douglasii) beneath them, ABOVE RIGHT, *steals the show. A stream, crossed by bridges,* BELOW RIGHT, *winds past flowers of* Darmera peltata *or* Peltiphyllum peltatum, CENTER, *and cow parsnip* (Heracleum lanatum), ABOVE.

THE EXQUISITE CLIMATE OF California represents different things to different people. To farmers, it's a land of nearly un-limited agricultural potential; to gardeners, it is a paradise found, where nearly any plant can sur-vive outdoors—providing there isn't a five-year drought. To nat-uralists and native-plant lovers, California is the last Eden, though an endangered one. The incredible diversity of the plants in the land west of the Rockies is staggering, and the many habi-tats within the state and niches within them present both oppor-tunity and challenge.

"One thing that grows won-derfully in one place won't do well ten miles away," says Ron Lutsko, who is noted for creating natural landscapes throughout the state, including the redesign of the Arthur L. Menzies Me-morial Garden in Golden Gate Park's Strybing Arboretum, San Francisco. The four-acre Menzies garden is a condensed look at that wide range of California's possibilities—and it won Lutsko the National Award of Merit from the American Society of Landscape Architects in 1991.

The Strybing Arboretum, of which Menzies is just a part, is dedicated to plants suited to what is called a "Mediterranean" cli-mate, with low rainfall, hot days, and cool nights—the kind of general conditions experienced in much of California. The four-acre Menzies garden, however, is planted purely in California na-tives—846 species. But unfor-tunately, there are few such enforced protected areas as Men-zies, and indigenous species have been pushed out by similar plants

zies' heroic gardener, King Sip.

Late fall is the beginning of her crew's busy time, when faded grasses are cut back into tuffets, their tops raked and collected with the rest of the season's debris. A burn would be helpful, but it is highly unlikely that it could take place in this town. Weeding of the meadow is probably three quarters of the work.

In winter, Sip makes three sowings of the native annuals that form the visual amalgam of the colorful plantings. The meadow foam, in particular, is a knitter, with cheerful yellow and white blossoms that can still be seen when the grasses are cut back. In time, Sip hopes, the annuals will self-sow with enough regularity to make them permanent members of this ever-evolving community.

The Menzies is one of a very few gardens that attempts to interpret some of the plant communities of a place as huge and diverse as California. The fact that it can teach so much in a relatively small place is miraculous. The fact that this has been done so beautifully is the pleasure of visiting this garden. It is a prototype for what botanical gardens should do, and what American gardeners can learn to do, too.

LEFT: *The view across the meadow to the aspen grove.*
OPPOSITE, CLOCKWISE FROM BOTTOM LEFT: *Chaparral is represented by shrubs and subshrubs; the bunchgrass meadow features pink Pacific Coast mallow (Sidalcea malviflora); rushes, sedges, and grasses such as Juncus patens, Carex fissuricola, and Calamagrostis nutkaensis; meadow flowers.*

Autumn at the Menzies.
OPPOSITE, CLOCKWISE
FROM BOTTOM LEFT:
California fuchsia
(Zauschneria cana);
*detail; yellow-twig
dogwood* (Cornus stolonifera
or C. sericea *'Flaviramea'*);
rush (Juncus patens); *Saint-
Catherine's-Lace*
(Eriogonum giganteum),
*native to Santa Catalina and
San Clemente islands; the
view across the meadow to the
aspen in fall; the silvery bark
shimmers when they become
the focal point of the garden
as winter approaches.*
OVERLEAF: *The winter
rains fill the arroyos that run
through the bunchgrass
meadow and produce the
spring explosion that plant
collections manager Barbara
Keller considers the crescendo
of the garden year. Then
the water pools in a basin
of cattails surrounded by
meadow foam.*

SOURCE GUIDE

PROPAGATION PRIMER

One of the better ways to acquire plants for your natural habitat garden is to buy them from native-plant societies. As nearly every state has a society, and nearly every society has one or more sales a year, the plants you desire may be available. These plants are usually donated by members who have propagated their own wildflowers. The other great way to get plants is to raise your own. Of course, you should never take plants from the wild. It is acceptable to rescue them when their habitats are threatened, from development sites, for example, provided you first secure permission.

Cultivars—cultivated varieties—selections, or forms cannot reproduce identical plants sexually. They must be propagated asexually, or vegetatively: from stem or root cuttings or by dividing clumps or rootstock. In the very near future, these plants may be propagated commercially by meristem tissue culture in vitro. In this method, cells from the shoot tip of a plant's stem are grown in test tubes or flasks on a sterile medium in laboratories with controlled temperatures. Entire plants, and thousands of them, each one identical to its parent, can be grown from these tiny tip cuttings.

Meristem reproduction is out of the gardener's reach, but even reproducing woody plants takes diligence and practice. Cuttings of fast-growing shrubs and trees tend to root more easily than ones that live for many years, such as tulip poplars (*Liriodendron tulipifera*), which are started from seed. Cultivars of trees have to be started from cuttings. A variegated dogwood might be grafted to its non-variegated "parent" species. Another dogwood may be easy to start from hard or softwood cuttings—last season's hardened woody growth, or new succulent growth. Silky dogwood (*Cornus amomum*) is a wetland plant that can be started from hard or soft cuttings or from seeds. Pagoda dogwood (*Cornus alternifolia*), on the other hand, can be started from seeds that have been exposed to five months

of warm temperatures followed by three months of cold treatment—an arduous process. This dogwood's cuttings must be of softwood, and also have to be dipped in a rooting hormone: powders or liquids that are available in several strengths for use on slips of plants of varying difficulty to root. Cut ends are dipped into the preparation and then placed in the rooting medium. Often these cuttings are also put in a propagation box and are misted with water nearly continuously to maintain lower temperatures in warm weather and keep moisture in the tissues. Some seeds and cuttings are also given heat from below to speed rooting. These operations are not easily tackled by hobbyists.

The least expensive, and perhaps most thrilling, method of starting wildflowers is from seed—either collected or purchased. It is easiest just to sow the seeds in protected beds outdoors. A cold frame might be the next best thing, but the process can be done indoors. In general, gathering some small portion of seed from substantial stands of plants will not threaten their existence. When you succeed, you will actually be contributing to their distribution, habitat, and survival. We subscribe to the ethical approach known as "conservation through propagation." If this is one of your first attempts, start with plants on your own property, or at least begin with a small experiment. Please don't collect seeds when there are only a few plants, or at the wrong time of year since this will result in failure. An artful propagator can actually improve upon nature's odds. You can often judge the ease at which a plant can reproduce from seed in the wild by the number of seeds produced.

Seeds are collected just as they ripen —just before they drop off the plant or are about to be dispersed by whatever the means the plant employs. Milkweed sends its seeds aloft on parachutes of silky fluff. Trillium fruits fall to the ground where ants often carry them away to partake of the fleshy cream-colored arils that run along the side of the seeds of many plants. Birds pick bite-sized berries

and the seeds pass through undigested —an excellent evolutionary distribution technique. When you locate some plants that you would like to grow in your garden, take careful notes. Record the date and the location, the streets and roads and any landmarks —even telephone poles—so you can return when the seeds are ripe. This can happen soon after flowering or after several months depending on the species—often when the seed capsules or pods turn brown.

Some plants look pretty shabby by the time the seeds are ready for harvest. In these cases, you might want to mark them with labels or flags. If you suspect that you will not be able to return on the exact day for a plant that has small seeds or capsules that explode to scatter the seeds, such as violets, then consider tying a tiny gauze bag over the just-faded flower. Take a square of the fabric, roll it up around the fertilized flower and tie it with thread at the top, above the flower, and the bottom, below it around the stem.

If the seeds have a dry, crusty casing, such as those of the composites, they should be separated or cleaned by rubbing them on a sieve or screen. If seeds come in a capsule, such as the mallows (*Hibiscus* spp.), simply invert the pods and tap the seeds out and into an envelope or shake onto clean newspaper. If the seeds are encased in a fruit, such as in the case of the maypop or passion flower (*Passiflora incarnata*), they have to be removed from ripe fruits and thoroughly cleaned. Most plants' fruits are ripe when they turn color. In the case of the maypop, the passion fruits, which are about the same shape as chicken eggs, turn from green to yellow.

Removing the seeds from fruits is not always an easy task. Cut large fruits carefully. Berries won't have to be cut. Hold the fruit pieces or berries over a sieve and rinse it under running warm water while squeezing the seeds free of the flesh. Always wash your hands after this process, and wash any implements that will be used for food preparation. Another suggestion is a twenty-four-hour soak in warm water, which softens the fruit and often separates it from the seeds. One method involves an actual fermentation of the fruit in water until the flesh rots off—several days. This might be specified for seeds that either go through the gastral tract of animals before sprouting or rely on microorganisms to clean the fruit away.

In general, all seeds should be sown in the medium soon after collection. If you need to store seeds, place them in clean, dry airtight containers, such as jars, in temperatures between 35 and 42 degrees Fahrenheit. That just happens to be the temperature of a refrigerator. Thirty-five-millimeter film canisters make good holders for little seeds and also are handy for collection in the field; just be sure to label all containers with the plant's name and the date on masking tape with a permanent marker and refrigerate. It is best not to store more than one kind of seed in any container. Some seeds can be stored for a year or more.

There are a few methods for sowing hardy wildflower seeds. Unlike the technique for planting tropical annual flowers or vegetables from seed, hardy plants will have to experience a treatment that simulates the conditions where they are found in the wild. Often, when a plant comes from a cold climate, their seeds must also be exposed to cold in order to germinate. Some seeds require cold periods followed by warmth and then cold again: double dormancy. These seeds could be sown directly into nursery beds in the outdoor garden to experience the natural processes. Or, to speed up the procedure, they can be stratified. That is a technique in which seeds are subjected to the necessary cold. After they have been sown in the planting medium, containers are placed in the refrigerator for the minimum amount of time necessary. Most seeds like this can be fooled into "thinking" they've been through a winter after about sixty days. Then you can place the seeds in a greenhouse, cold frame, very sunny window, or under fluorescent lights for germination.

Some plants have very hard seed coats that are often nibbled by animals, allowing moisture to get inside. In nature, the seed coats might also be broken into by microbes or cracked from seasons of freezing and thawing. These seeds can be scarified. This amounts to nicking the seeds with a sharp knife or filing a groove in the side for water to get in. Small seeds can be rolled between two sheets of sandpaper. You might also try soaking the seeds for twenty-four hours in warm water—this works for some seeds—even with very hard coats, such as the legume bush pea (*Thermopsis villosa*). Bluestar (*Amsonia tabernaemontana*) has to be scarified *and* soaked overnight.

Jack-in-the-pulpits are easy wildflowers to start from seed. In late summer, berries arranged tightly on a stalk formed by the female plants turn brilliant scarlet-orange. Plants can be Jacks or Jills depending on the conditions of the location—usually being female in good seasons when soils are adequately fertile. To start jack-in-the-pulpits, I clean the seeds and store them dry or in their sowing medium in the refrigerator for sixty days. However, these seeds have even germinated when I just picked the entire fruit cluster, refrigerated it for sixty days, and cleaned and sowed the seeds.

I sow the jack-in-the-pulpit seeds in a moistened commercial "peat-lite" starting mix (ground peat moss and perlite and/or vermiculite). For acid-loving woodland plants, add one part peat moss to each part peat-lite mix and an additional amount of clean, coarse sand. If parent plants come from dry soil areas add extra sand—up to three parts to every part peat-lite mix. Waterside plants can be sown in peat-lite mix in containers set half deep in water.

Plant most seeds to a depth that equals its thickness. Very fine seed is sprinkled on the surface of the medium. Little seeds need light to germinate. Once sown, seeds should never be allowed to dry. The peat-lite medium becomes pale-colored as it dries. You can water containers with large seeds, such as the Jacks, from the top, but small seeds should be watered when necessary by putting their containers in deep saucers of water until the top of the medium is moist so as not to dislodged them with the force of the water. (If you are sowing in nursery beds outside, account for the force of raindrops on fine seed. You'll have to protect these as well with a lean-to of plastic or other transparent covering. They will have to rely on you for watering.)

I place up to a dozen seeds in a three-inch pot. Seedlings will be separated to individual containers once they have their second set of leaves. The pots of jack-in-the-pulpits, placed in saucers or trays, are arranged with the pot rim about eight inches below two four-foot-long fluorescent tubes (forty watts each). As the plants sprout, in only three to four weeks for the Jacks, the pots will be lowered to maintain an eight-inch distance from the top of the seedlings' leaves. Plants demanding more light—those not from the woodland but from sunny meadows, for example, would be placed as close as four inches away from the lights. The lights can be placed on a timer so that they burn sixteen hours each day. The entire light fixture and trays are covered with a plastic drop cloth to maintain high humidity during the process.

Everything must be as clean as possible. I have even baked the planting mix in the oven at around 250 degrees Fahrenheit for an hour (garden soil treated this way will be sterilized but may have a foul odor).

In early spring, I will place the seedlings outdoors after a period of hardening-off. If you have a shaded cold frame, even an inexpensive plastic affair, you can place the potted seedlings right inside it at this time. Just be sure to open the frame for ventilation on warm days. Otherwise, place the seedlings outdoors in a sheltered spot for one hour the first day, two the next, and so on until about a week, when they can be left outdoors. You may want to keep the little plants in pots until their second year, or plant them in the fall when they have grown a bit. If you keep them in pots for a winter, bury the pots to their rims and apply a loose mulch of pine boughs after the ground is frozen. This is a great way to recycle the Christmas tree (sans tinsel).

See the following list for information on native-plant propagation:

Bir, Richard E. *Growing and Propagating Showy Native Woody Plants*. Chapel Hill: The University of North Carolina Press, 1992.

Curtis, Will C., revised by William E. Brumback. *Propagation of Wildflowers*. Framingham, Mass.: The New England Wild Flower Society, 1986.

Phillips, Harry R. *Growing and Propagating Wildflowers*. Chapel Hill: The University of North Carolina Press, 1985.

INTEGRATED PEST MANAGEMENT (IPM)

Conventional horticulture has traditionally recommended a regular preventive spray schedule for gardens. Likewise, green grass lawn was thought to be dependent on tons of water, herbicides, and fertilizer. The promise for natural habitat gardening lies in something called Integrated Pest Management (IPM), an enlightened approach for controlling diseases, weeds, and insects in the garden, farm, and even the home, which advocates a series of decision-making steps to arrive at the least-toxic solution possible. Soon these unfamiliar initials will be as well-known as the letters of their biological antithesis, DDT. We may not have any choice. More farm and garden chemicals are being banned every year.

IPM's step-by-step approach begins by not planting "incorrectly." Plants that are in stressful situations because of improper siting are the ones most likely to succumb to problems. When a plant has evolved to cope with the conditions in a certain area, then, obviously, it will be the best choice for that place. Taking IPM to its ultimate conclusion—the most surefire solution of all—*don't plant the wrong plant in the wrong place.*

Sanitation is extremely important, as both a prevention and a control. Remove damaged leaves, and continue to monitor the problem. See what can be done culturally. Reducing the desirability of the environment for a given pest is a good way to limit its effects. In the case of mildew, keeping garden hose spray off the leaves will help. Attempt to improve air circulation by removing obstacles, such as solid fences, or trimming overgrown shrubs. Then comes diligent observation.

New products will come out. In all cases, and with the use of any product, *read the label* carefully and thoroughly for the manufacturer's recommended rates, methods and schedules of applications, and warnings or cautions. Even safe products might damage the leaves of some plants if used at the wrong time.

When it comes to insects, the stepped approach continues with an unappealing environment—using insect-resistant cultivars, for example. Then there's hand picking—remove individual insects as they are discovered; if the problem will get out of control without more serious intervention, there are barriers, such as netting. Sometimes traps are used: some with synthetic pheromones (sex attractors), or those baited with fragrant lures that resemble the insect's favorite meal. Place these traps upwind and as far away from the host plant as possible. You could place a beetle trap, for example, with its collection bag removed, over the stocked pool or pond. Beetles fly toward it and crash into the yellow trap and fall into the water to be gobbled up.

Other visual devices, such as sticky red balls to hang in crab apple trees early in the season, attract and catch apple-maggot flies. Sticky yellow flags are effective for houseplants and ornamentals outdoors. Yellow draws many flying insects; it works, just like old-fashioned flypaper.

There are biological controls, too—germ warfare on pests. In the 1970s, many people sprayed poisons for gypsy moths, but some enlightened home owners realized that spraying would throw off the balance of nature by starving the moths' natural predators. Eventually, nature's balance would prevail. In the wet summer of 1990, a naturally occurring fungal disease had the gypsy caterpillars dropping like flies.

Certain pathogens can be easily introduced. *Bacillus thuringiensis,* called Bt, can be bought at the garden center as a powder or a liquid. This is a bacterial disease that kills nearly all caterpillars, but will not harm adults of the same species, or other insects for that matter. It sounds like germ warfare (it is). But this selective bacillus will not harm anything else. Certain insects have been able to develop immunity to some of these new bacilli. New host-specific remedies are becoming available every year. (There is now one called *Bacillus thuringiensis israelensis* that controls mosquitoes.)

As with every new trend, entrepreneurs saw an opportunity for profit. You've probably seen ads in catalogs and garden magazines for praying mantis egg cases to "rid your garden of pests." It's a tempting idea. Who can resist something as natural as three hundred baby chewing machines hatching among the branches of your very own rhododendron? But praying mantes are not acceptable IPM predators—they are indiscriminate consumers. They will eat anything that moves, including their brethren.

Another irresistible offering is the "cup-o-ladybugs." Some entomologists warn that although the ladybugs eat all manner of nasty critters, it isn't as easy as sprinkling a few dozen out of the container in which they arrived. Ladybugs are collected as they sleep through dormancy in their mountain homes. In nature, they wake up and fly away. When you buy ladybugs, they wake up and flee. Occasionally you'll find one in your garden and think how successful you've been, but this is probably a local resident. Ladybugs *can* be brought to the garden, but usually they have to be captured and shipped in their "wake-up-and-eat" stage—not an easy task.

You might have to turn to a naturally derived toxin or a degradable fatty-acid soap, for example, that will not harm the environment. And these are pest-specific, that is, they kill only the invader and leave the beneficial insects, family members, pets, and produce alone. Whenever curatives are called for, aim directly at the problem area, in a pinpoint spray, and never broadcast all over creation.

When all else fails, more severe measures may be taken. Dormant oil spray can be used when plants are not in active growth and pests are in their rest cycle. This material will smother the problem insect, such as scale, without harming either the tree or other insects that do not hibernate in this manner. Botanical pesticides derived from plants such as rotenone, pyrethrum, ryania, neem, sabadilla, and nicotine are real poisons; nicotine sulfate, for example, is toxic to mammals. But they break down rapidly, unlike synthetic insecticides. Sorptive dusts, such as boric acid, sodium bicarbonate, silica gel, and diatomaceous earth, work by destroying the protective wax or mucous coating of many insects. However, care should be taken to avoid inhaling the dusts or rubbing the eyes, and always stand upwind. Again, read the label and only apply to the affected areas.

Some of the safe materials, such as baking soda, might be nearly as unsightly as the mildew it is used to control, but that's okay, too. We're more than happy to put up with a few imperfections if we can end the cases of illness and even death from careless use of pesticides. The garden will never be completely pest-free, so plant extra lettuce for the critters.

NURSERIES

Today there are many nurseries that make native plants available to professional and amateur gardeners. Assembled here are the names and addresses of mail-order suppliers of wildflowers, both plants and seeds. To the best of our ability, we have checked to make sure that all of these sources propagate their offerings and never wild-collect. You might want to start by writing for lists and catalogs from companies in your area that will probably experience many of the same habitat conditions as you have on your site. For this purpose, the following list is arranged by state. When you see (d) after an entry, it means that the cost of the catalog is deductible from the first order. If you are testing the quality of a supplier, place a small order, or share an order with friends. Soon, you will become familiar with reliable growers who are also comrades in our quest to repopulate our gardens and our landscapes with natives. Many of these devoted nursery owners will become invaluable sources of plant information, and in time will become friends as well.

ALASKA

BALDWIN SEED CO. OF ALASKA
PO Box 3127
Kenai, AK 99611-3127
(906) 262-2285
Wildflower seeds. Catalog $1.50

ARIZONA

SOUTHWESTERN NATIVE SEEDS
Box 50503
Tucson, AZ 85703
Native flower seeds, trees, shrubs, wildflowers. Catalog $1

ARKANSAS

HOLLAND WILDFLOWER FARM
290 O'Neal Lane
Elkins, AR 72727
(800) 752-5079 or
(501) 643-2622
Wildflower plants and seeds. Catalog $1.50

CALIFORNIA

BAY VIEW GARDENS
1201 Bay Street
Santa Cruz, CA 95060
(408) 423-3656
Pacific Coast native iris. Catalog $1.50

CLYDE ROBIN SEED COMPANY
PO Box 2366
Castro Valley, CA 94546
(415) 581-3468
Wildflower seeds. Catalog $2

LARNER SEEDS
PO Box 407, 235 Fern Road
Bolinas, CA 94924
(415) 868-9407
Native Western seeds. Catalog $2

LAS PILITAS NURSERY
Las Pilitas Road
Santa Margarita, CA 93453
(805) 438-5992
Native seeds and plants. Catalog $4

MOON MOUNTAIN
PO Box 34
Morro Bay, CA 93443
(805) 772-2473
Wildflower seeds. Catalog $2

WILDWOOD FARM
10300 Sonoma Highway
Kenwood, CA 95452
Drought-tolerant plants

COLORADO

COLORADO ALPINES, INC.
PO Box 2708
Avon, CO 81620
(303) 949-6464 or 6672
Alpines and miniature plants. Catalog $2

EDGE OF THE ROCKIES
133 Hunna Road
Bayfield, CO 81122-9758
Plants and seeds; native wildflowers, trees, and shrubs; grasses. Catalog $1

OLD FARM NURSERY
5550 Indiana Street
Golden, CO 80403
(303) 278-0754 or 0755
Native plants

ROCKY MOUNTAIN RARE PLANTS
PO Box 200483
Denver, CO 80220-0483
Native plant seeds of the Rocky Mountains, and exotics

SHARP BROS. SEED CO.
101 East 4th Street Road
Greely, CO 80631
(303) 356-4710
Wildflower and native grass seeds

WESTERN NATIVE SEED
PO Box 1281
Canon City, CO 81215
(719) 275-8414
Wildflower seeds. Catalog $1

WILD & CRAZY SEED CO.
PO Box 895
Durango, CO 83102
(303) 259-6385
Wildflower seeds

FLORIDA

BLAKE'S NURSERY
Route 2, Box 971, Highway 90 East
Madison, FL 32340
(904) 971-5003
Native trees and shrubs

GEORGIA

ECO-GARDENS
PO Box 1227
Decatur, GA 30031
(404) 294-6468
Native Eastern wildflowers, trees, shrubs, ferns, and exotics

WILDWOOD FARMS
5231 Seven Islands Road
Madison, GA 30650
(706) 342-4912
Native trees, shrubs, vines, and perennials

IDAHO

NATIVE SEED FOUNDATION
Star Route
Moyie Springs, ID 83845
(208) 267-7938
Native tree and shrub seeds and some young plants

SEEDS TRUST–HIGH ALTITUDE GARDENS
PO Box 4619
Ketchum, ID 83340
(208) 726-3221
Wildflower and native grass seeds

SILVER SPRINGS NURSERY
HCR 62, Box 86
Moyie Springs, ID 83845
(208) 267-5753
Native ground covers

ILLINOIS

AVID GARDENER
Springvale Farm Nursery Inc.
Mozier Hollow Road
Hamburg, IL 62045
(618) 232-1108
Rare conifers, many North American natives

BLUESTEM PRAIRIE NURSERY
Ken Schaal
Rural Route 2, Box 92
Hillsboro, IL 62049
(217) 532-6344
Native Illinois wildflower plants and seeds

GENESIS NURSERY
Route 1, Box 32
Walnut, IL 61376
(815) 379-9060
Plants and seeds; wildflowers, grasses, trees, and shrubs

LAFAYETTE HOME NURSERY, INC.
LaFayette, IL 61449-9702
(309) 995-3311
Grasses, sedges, forbs, woody plant seeds, wildflower seeds

MIDWEST WILDFLOWERS
Box 64
Rockton, IL 61072
Wildflower seeds native to the Midwest

IOWA

ALLENDAN SEED
Route 4, Box 625
Winterset, IA 50273
(515) 462-1241
Native grass seeds

IOWA PRAIRIE SEED COMPANY
RR 1, Box 259
Cresco, IA 52136
(319) 547-3824
Wildflower seeds

KANSAS

SHARP BROS. SEED CO.
Box 140
Healy, KS 67850
(316) 398-2231, or
(800) 4-NATIVE
Wildflower and native grass seeds

KENTUCKY

SHOOTING STAR NURSERY
444 Bates Road
Frankfort, KY 40601
(502) 223-1679
Seeds and propagated plants; wildflowers, grasses, sedges, rushes, shrubs, woody vines, ground covers, and trees

LOUISIANA

LOUISIANA NURSERY
Route 7, Box 43
Opelousas, LA 70570
(318) 948-3696
Wildflowers, grass seed, trees, and shrubs, especially magnolias. Catalog $5

NATIVES NURSERIES
320 North Theard Street
Covington, LA 70433
(504) 892-5424
Trees and shrubs

MAINE

EASTERN NATIVE PLANT SPECIALISTS
Box 226
Georgetown, Maine 04548
(207) 371-2888
Rare woodland and native New England plants

FIELDSTONE GARDENS, INC.
620 Quaker Lane
Vassalboro, ME 04989-9713
(207) 923-3836
Perennials: familiar and rare. Catalog $1.50

MARYLAND

CROWNSVILLE NURSERY
PO Box 797
Crownsville, MD 21032
(301) 923-2212
Ornamental perennials, natives, excellent quality. Catalog $2 (d)

ENVIRONMENTAL CONCERN, INC.
PO Box P
210 West Chew Avenue
St. Michaels, MD 21663
(410) 745-9620
Native wetland plants

INDIGO KNOLL PERENNIALS
16236 Compromise Court
Mt. Airy, MD 21771
(301) 489-5131
Border and rock garden plants, native herbs

KURT BLEUMEL, INC.
2740 Green Lane
Baldwin, MD 21013
(301) 557-7229
Exotic and some native ornamental grasses, rushes, sedges, aquatics, wildflowers. Catalog $2

MARYLAND AQUATIC NURSERIES
3427 North Furnace Road
Jarrettsville, MD 21084
(301) 557-7615
Native bog and water plants and others. Catalog $2

MASSACHUSETTS

DONAROMA'S NURSERY
PO Box 2189
Upper Main Street
Edgartown, MA 02539
(508) 627-8366 or 3036
Wildflowers and ornamental perennials. Catalog $3

SEEDS NEW ENGLAND WILD FLOWER SOCIETY, INC.
Garden in the Woods
180 Hemenway Road
Framingham, MA 01701-2699
Catalog $2

WYRTTUN WARD
18 Beach Street
Middleboro, MA 02346
Woodland wildflowers. Catalog $1

MICHIGAN

THE MICHIGAN WILDFLOWER FARM
11770 Cutler Road
Portland, MI 48875-9452
(517) 647-6010
Native wildflower seeds

OWL RIDGE ALPINES
5421 Whipple Lake Road
Clarkston, MI 48016
Alpine and woodland species

MINNESOTA

FEDER'S PRAIRIE SEED CO.
Route 1, Box 41
Blue Earth, MN 56013
(507) 526-3049
Seeds, wildflowers, grasses

LANDSCAPE ALTERNATIVES, INC.
1465 North Pascal Street
St. Paul, MN 55108
(612) 488-3142
Wildflowers, wildflower seeds, grass seeds. Catalog $1

PRAIRIE MOON NURSERY
Alan Wade
Route 3, Box 163
Winona, MN 55987
(507) 452-1362 or 5231
Native forbs, shrubs, vines, grasses, and sedges; seeds and plants. Catalog $2

PRAIRIE RESTORATIONS, INC.
PO Box 327
Princeton, MN 55371
(612) 389-4342
Minnesota native wildflowers and grasses; mail order within a 200-mile radius

RICE CREEK GARDENS, INC.
11506 Highway 65
Blaine, MN 55432
(612) 754-8090
Wildflowers. Catalog $2

MISSISSIPPI

SOUTHERN PERENNIALS & HERBS
Route 3, Box 174-G
Tylertown, MS 39667
(601) 684-1769
Wildflowers, grasses, and herbs, some nonnatives; plants

MISSOURI

HAMILTON SEEDS AND WILDFLOWERS
HC Route 9, Box 138
Elk Creek, MO 65464
(417) 967-2190
Wildflowers, wildflower seeds, grass seeds, and trees

MISSOURI WILDFLOWERS
9814 Pleasant Hill Road
Jefferson City, MO 65109
(314) 496-3492
Native perennials, seeds, and plants. Catalog $1

SHARP BROS. SEED CO.
Route 4, Box 237A
Clinton, MO 64735
(816) 885-7551 or
(800) 451-3779
Wildflower and native grass seeds

MONTANA

FOUR WINDS NURSERY
5853 East Shore Route
Polson, MT 59860
(406) 887-2215
Montana native plants

WILD FLOWER SEEDS
Ruth Unger
630 Wildlife Lane
Anaconda, MT 59711
(406) 563-8048
Seeds; wildflowers, grasses, trees, and shrubs. Catalog $1

NEBRASKA

AURORA McTURF
PO Box 194
Aurora, NE 68818
(308) 381-7092
Native grass seeds

THE FRAGRANT PATH
PO Box 328
Fort Calhoun, NE 68023
Some native prairie grasses, and forbs. Catalog $1

PAUL E. ALLEN FARM SUPPLY
Route 2, Box 8
Bristow, NE 68719-9407
(402) 583-9924
Wildflower seeds

STOCK SEED FARMS
28008 Mill Road
Murdock, NE 68407-2350
(402) 867-3771 or
(800) 759-1520
Prairie grass and wildflower seeds

NEW JERSEY

LOFT SEED, INC.
Attn. Research
PO Box 146
Bound Brook, NJ 08805
(908) 560-1590
Some native ornamental grasses and wildflower seeds

NEW MEXICO

BERNARDO BEACH NATIVE PLANT FARM
1 Sanchez Road
Veguita, NM 87062
Various plants of the Southwest. Catalog $1 (d)

CURTIS AND CURTIS SEED AND SUPPLY, INC.
Star Route Box 8-A
Clovis, NM 88101
(505) 762-4759
Native grass seeds

DESERT MOON NURSERY
PO Box 600
Veguita, NM 87062
(505) 864-0614
Wildflowers, trees, shrubs, succulents, and cacti (all propagated). Catalog $1

PLANTS OF THE SOUTHWEST
930 Baca Street
Santa Fe, NM 87501
(505) 983-1548
Plants and seeds; wildflowers, grasses, trees, and shrubs. Catalog $1.50

NEW YORK

BOTANIC GARDEN COMPANY
9 Wycoff Street
Brooklyn, NY 11201
(718) 624-8839
Wildflower seeds

ST. LAWRENCE NURSERIES
RD 2, Route 345, Potsdam-Madrid Road
Potsdam, NY 13676
(315) 265-6739
Cold-hardy fruit and nut trees

WILDGINGER WOODLANDS
PO Box 1091
Webster, NY 14580
*Wildflower seeds and plants.
Catalog $1 (d)*

NORTH CAROLINA

ARROWHEAD NURSERY
Watia Road, Box 38
Bryson City, NC 28713
(704) 488-6840
Some native trees and shrubs

BOOTHE HILL WILDFLOWER
SEEDS AND PLANTS
23B Boothe Hill Road
Chapel Hill, NC 27514
(919) 967-4091
*Native and some nonnative
plants and seeds*

BROOKSIDE WILDFLOWERS
Route 3, Box 740
Boone, NC 28607
(704) 963-5548
Wildflower plants

FERN VALLEY FARMS
US 421 Service Road East
Route 4, Box 235
Yadkinville, NC 27055
(919) 463-2412
*Propagated trees, shrubs, and
ferns native to the Carolinas*

HOLBROOK FARM
115 Lance Road
PO Box 368
Fletcher, NC 28732-0368
(704) 891-7790
*Perennials, wildflowers, woody
plants, and grasses*

HUFFMAN'S NATIVE PLANTS
PO Box 39
Otto, NC 28763
(704) 524-7446
*Seeds; woody plants. Catalog
SASE*

HUNGRY PLANTS
1216 Cooper Drive
Raleigh, NC 27607
(919) 851-6521
*Native wetland carnivorous
plants. Catalog SASE*

LAMTREE FARM
Route 1, Box 162
Warrensville, NC 28693
(919) 385-6144 or
(800) 537-5268
*Native propagated shrubs, trees,
and perennials; some nonnatives*

NICHE GARDENS
1111 Dawson Road
Chapel Hill, NC 27516
(919) 967-0078
*Nursery propagated natives,
especially Southeast herbaceous
plants, trees, and shrubs*

PLANT DELIGHTS NURSERY
9241 Sauls Road
Raleigh, NC 27603
(919) 772-4794
*Dedicated newcomers geared to
plant "junkies." Catalog $2*

THE SANDY MUSH
HERB NURSERY
Route 2, Surrett Cove Road
Leicester, NC 28748
(704) 683-2014
*Herbs, grasses, shrubs,
wildflowers, perennials.
Catalog $4*

WE-DU NURSERIES
Route 5, Box 724
Marion, NC 28752
(704) 738-8300
*Woodland plants.
Catalog $1 (d)*

THE WILDWOOD FLOWER
Route 3, Box 165
Pittsboro, NC 27312
(919) 542-4344
*Wildflowers, some woody
shrubs and ferns; specializes in
Lobelia species and cultivars;
plants. Catalog SASE*

OHIO

COMPANION PLANTS
7247 North Coolville
Ridge Road
Athens, OH 45701
(614) 592-4643
*Mostly herbs, some native
plants. Catalog $2*

MARY'S PLANT FARM
2410 Lanes Mill Road
Hamilton, OH 45013
(513) 892-2055 or 894-0022
*Native perennials, ferns,
flowering shrubs, and trees;
shade-tolerant plants.
Catalog $1 (d)*

VALLEY CREEK, INC.
PO Box 475, Circle Drive
McArthur, OH 45651
(614) 596-2521
Wildflower seeds

OREGON

CALLAHAN SEEDS
6045 Foley Lane
Central Point, OR 97502
(503) 855-1164
Western trees and shrubs

FORESTFARM
990 Tetherow Road
Williams, OR 97544
(503) 846-6963
*Excellent source of woody
natives and unusual plants;
informative catalog; one of the
best sources. Catalog $3*

GREER GARDENS
1280 Goodpasture
Island Road
Eugene, OR 97401-1794
(503) 686-8266
*Rhododendrons, azaleas, trees,
shrubs, rock gardens, ground
covers. Catalog $3*

RUSSELL GRAHAM
4030 Eagle Crest Road, NW
Salem, OR 97304
(503) 362-1135
*Hardy perennials, native
plants, hardy ferns, ornamental
grasses*

SISKIYOU RARE
PLANT NURSERY
2825 Cummings Road
Medford, OR 97501
(503) 772-6846
*Incredible selection of wild
plants; specializing in, but not
limited to, alpines and rock
garden plants. Catalog $2 (d)*

PENNSYLVANIA

APPALACHIAN GARDENS
PO Box 82
Waynesboro, PA 17268
(717) 762-4312
Rare plants, hardy ornamentals

APPALACHIAN WILDFLOWER
NURSERY
Route 1, Box 275A
Honey Creek Road
Reedsville, PA 17084
(717) 667-6998
*Plants native to the New Jersey
Pine Barrens, Soviet Union,
Caucasus. Catalog $2 (d)*

BOWMAN'S HILL
WILDFLOWER PRESERVE
Washington Crossing
Historic Park
PO Box 103
Washington Crossing, PA
18977
(215) 862-2924
Pennsylvania native seeds

THE PRIMROSE PATH
RD 2, Box 110
Scottdale, PA 15683
(412) 887-6756
*Woodland plants and other
perennials. Catalog $2 (d)*

ZETTS FISH FARM AND
HATCHERIES
Drifting, PA 16834
(814) 345-5357
*Live fish, aquatic animals, and
plants*

SOUTH CAROLINA

COASTAL GARDENS
& NURSERY
4611 Socastee Boulevard
Myrtle Beach, SC 29575
(803) 293-2000
*Ornamental grasses, ferns,
perennials: participates in
worldwide seed exchange.
Catalog $2 (d)*

OAK HILL FARM
204 Pressly Street
Clover, SC 29710-1233
(803) 222-4245
Native trees and shrubs

WOODLANDERS, INC.
1128 Colleton Avenue
Aiken, SC 29801
(803) 648-7522
*Native trees and shrubs,
grasses, ferns, vines, herbaceous
perennials. Catalog $2*

TENNESSEE

BEAVER CREEK NURSERY
7526 Pelleaux Road
Knoxsville, TN 37938
(615) 922-3961
*Rare and unusual plants.
Catalog 45 cents*

BEERSHEBA WILDFLOWER
GARDEN
PO Box 551
Stone Door Road
Beersheba Springs, TN
37305
(615) 692-3575
*Hardy native perennial
wildflowers and ferns*

NATIVE GARDENS
Meredith Bradford-Clebsch
and Ed Clebsch
5737 Fisher Lane
Greenback, TN 37742
(615) 856-3350
*Native forbs, ferns, grasses,
trees, shrubs, vines, perennials,
and herbs; plants and seeds.
Catalog $2*

NATURAL GARDENS
113 Jasper Lane
Oak Ridge, TN 37830
(615) 856-3350
*Native woodland and marsh
plants from the Southeast.
Catalog $1 (d)*

SUNLIGHT GARDENS, INC.
Route 1, Box 600-A,
Hillvale Road
Andersonville, TN 37705
(615) 494-8237
*Forbs, ferns, perennials, vines,
trees, shrubs of eastern North
America; plants; seeds by
special order only. Catalog $3*

TEXAS

GREEN HORIZONS
218 Quinlan #571
Kerrville, TX 78028
(210) 257-5141
*Wildflower and grass seeds.
Catalog SASE*

ROBINSON SEED CO.
1113 Jefferson Drive
Plainview, TX 79072
(806) 293-4959
Wildflower and grass seeds

SHARP BROS. SEED CO.
Route 9, Box 2
Amarillo, TX 79108
(806) 383-7772
*Wildflower and native grass
seeds*

WILDSEED, INC.
1101 Campo Rosa Road
PO Box 308
Eagle Lake, TX 77434
(409) 234-7353 in Texas,
(800) 848-0078 outside Texas
Wildflower seeds. Catalog $2

**YUCCA DO AND
PECKERWOOD GARDENS**
FM 359, PO Box 655
Waller, TX 77484
(409) 826-6363
*Native plants of the Southwest.
Very large collection of salvias.
Catalog $3*

VERMONT

VERMONT WILDFLOWER FARM
Dept. BK, Route 7
Charlotte, VT 05445-0005
(802) 425-3500
Wildflower seeds

VIRGINIA

VIRGINIA WILDE FARMS
Route 2, Box 1512
Hanover, VA 23069
(804) 643-0021
*Specializes in hardy native
plants for sunny locations and
plants with traditional medicinal
usage; trees, vines, shrubs, and
herbaceous wildflowers.
Catalog $2*

WASHINGTON

**ABUNDANT LIFE SEED
FOUNDATION**
PO Box 772, 1029 Lawrence
Port Townsend, WA 98368
(206) 385-5660
*Wildflowers, tree, and shrub
seed. Catalog $2*

**COLVOS CREEK NURSERY
& LANDSCAPING**
1931 Second Avenue, #215
Seattle, WA 98101
(206) 441-1509
*Unusual Pacific Coast natives.
Catalog $2 (d)*

FANCY FRONDS
1911 Fourth Avenue, W
Seattle, WA 98119
*Ferns from everywhere,
excellent source. Catalog $1 (d)*

FOLIAGE GARDENS
2003 128th Avenue, SE
Bellevue, WA 98005
(206) 747-2998
*Ferns: all spore-grown.
Catalog $2*

FROSTY HOLLOW NURSERY
PO Box 53
Langley, WA 98260
(206) 221-2332
*Specializes in ecological
restoration and rescues, and
propagates plants of Pacific
Northwest. Catalog SASE*

HERONSWOOD NURSERY
7530 288th, NE
Kingston, WA 98356
(206) 297-4172
*Large and detailed range of
unusual woody and herbaceous
plants. Catalog $3*

MCLAUGHLIN'S SEEDS
Buttercup's Acre
Mead, WA
99021-0550
(509) 466-0230
Wildflower seeds

PLANTS OF THE WILD
PO Box 866
Tekoa, WA 99033
(509) 284-2848
Container-grown native plants

WISCONSIN

**BOEHLKE'S WOODLAND
GARDENS**
W140N 10829 Country
Aire Rd.
Germantown, WI 53022
*Native marsh and woodland
perennials. Catalog $1*

**COUNTRY WETLANDS
NURSERY AND CONSULTING,
LTD.**
575 W20755 Field Drive
Muskego, WI 53150
(414) 679-1268
*Wetland plants, woodland
plants and seeds. Catalog $2*

**KESTER'S WILD GAME FOOD
NURSERIES, INC.**
PO Box 516
Omro, WI 54963
(414) 685-2929 or
(800) 558-8815
*Specializes in wildlife
plantings. Catalog $2*

LITTLE VALLEY FARM
Route 3, Box 544
Snead Creek Road
Spring Green, WI 53588
(608) 935-3324
*Native plants and seeds; shrubs,
vines, forbs, and trees for
prairie, wetland, and woodland*

NATURE'S NURSERY
6125 Mathewson Road
Mazomanie, WI 53560
(608) 795-4920
*Wildflowers, wildflower and
grass seeds*

PRAIRIE NURSERY
PO Box 306
Westfield, WI 53964
(608) 296-3679
*Wildflowers, grasses, seeds, and
plants. Catalog $3*

PRAIRIE RIDGE NURSERY
RR 2, 9738 Overland Road
Mt. Horeb, WI 53572-2832
(608) 437-5245
*Grasses, sedges, forbs; plants
and seeds for prairie, woodland,
and wetland. Catalog $2*

PRAIRIE SEED SOURCE
PO Box 83
North Lake, WI 53064-0083
*Southeastern Wisconsin grass,
shrub, and forb seeds*

WYOMING

WIND RIVER SEED, INC.
Route 1, Box 97
3075 Lane 51½
Manderson, WY 82432-9605
(307) 568-3325
*Wildflower, grass, tree, and
shrub seeds*

CANADA

NATURAL LEGACY SEEDS
RR 2C-1
Laird Armstrong, B.C.,
Canada V0E 1B0
*Native seeds for wildflowers,
grasses, ground covers,
shrubs, and trees*

NATIVE-PLANT
SOCIETIES

There are thousands of people who share your love of native plants. It's fun to join a society and communicate with members through newsletters and meetings. There are several societies dedicated to specific kinds of plants, such as carnivores, but for the most part, the list below includes general native-plant groups around the country. Keep in mind that these organizations have sales of plants propagated by members to raise funds. This is the best way to get indigenous plants for your habitat gardens. The California Native Plant Society's bulletin, for example, often lists as many as a dozen such sales around the state each month. In the East, you might plan to go the New England Wild Flower Society's yearly plant sale, usually held in June.

ALABAMA

**ALABAMA WILDFLOWER
SOCIETY**
c/o George Wood
11120 Ben Clements Road
Northport, AL 35476

ALASKA

**ALASKA NATIVE PLANT
SOCIETY**
PO Box 141613
Anchorage, AK 99514
(907) 333-8212

ARIZONA

**ARIZONA NATIVE PLANT
SOCIETY**
PO Box 41206
Tucson, AZ 85717

NATIVE SEEDS/SEARCH
2509 North Campbell
Avenue, #325
Tucson, AZ 85719
(602) 327-9123
Publishes fascinating quarterly

ARKANSAS

**ARKANSAS NATIVE PLANT
SOCIETY**
PO Box 250250
Little Rock, AR 72225

CALIFORNIA

CALIFORNIA NATIVE PLANT
SOCIETY
909 12th Street, Suite 116
Sacramento, CA 95814
(916) 447-2677

SOCIETY FOR PACIFIC COAST
NATIVE IRIS
977 Meredith Court
Sonoma, CA 95476

SOUTHERN CALIFORNIA
BOTANISTS
Dept. of Biology
Fullerton State University
Fullerton, CA 92634
(714) 449-7034

THE THEODORE PAYNE
FOUNDATION
10459 Tuxford Street
Sun Valley, CA 91352
(818) 768-1802

COLORADO

COLORADO NATIVE PLANT
SOCIETY
PO Box 200
Fort Collins, CO 80522

CONNECTICUT

CONNECTICUT BOTANICAL
SOCIETY, INC.
Osborn Memorial
Laboratory
167 Prospect Street
New Haven, CT 06511
(203) 388-6148

DISTRICT OF COLUMBIA

BOTANICAL SOCIETY OF
WASHINGTON
Dept of Botany, NHB/166
Smithsonian Institution
Washington, DC 20560

FLORIDA

THE FLORIDA NATIVE PLANT
SOCIETY
PO Box 680008
Orlando, FL 32868
(407) 299-1472

IDAHO

IDAHO NATIVE PLANT
SOCIETY
PO Box 9451
Boise, ID 83707

ILLINOIS

ILLINOIS NATIVE PLANT
SOCIETY
Forest Glen Preserve
RR 1, Box 495A
Westville, IL 61883
(217) 662-2142

SOUTHERN ILLINOIS NATIVE
PLANT SOCIETY
Botany Dept.
Southern Illinois University
Carbondale, IL 52901

INDIANA

A.N.V.I.L. (ASSOCIATION
FOR THE USE OF NATIVE
VEGETATION IN LANDSCAPE)
871 Shawnee Avenue
Lafayette, IN 47905

KANSAS

KANSAS WILDFLOWER
SOCIETY
Mulvane Art Center
Washburn University
Topeka, KS 66611
(913) 296-6324

SAVE THE TALLGRASS PRAIRIE,
INC.
4101 West 54th Terrace
Shawnee Mission, KS 66025

LOUISIANA

LOUISIANA NATIVE PLANT
SOCIETY
Route 1, Box 151
Saline, LA 71070

LOUISIANA PROJECT
WILDFLOWER
c/o Lafayette Natural
History Museum
637 Girard Park Drive
Lafayette, LA 70503
(318) 261-8350

SOCIETY OF LOUISIANA IRIS
PO Box 40175
Lafayette, LA 70504
(318) 264-6203

MARYLAND

CHESAPEAKE AUDUBON
SOCIETY
Rare Plant Committee
PO Box 3173
Baltimore, MD 21228

MASSACHUSETTS

NEW ENGLAND WILD
FLOWER SOCIETY
Garden in the Woods
180 Hemenway Road
Framingham, MA 01701-
2699
(508) 877-7630

MICHIGAN

MICHIGAN BOTANICAL CLUB
Matthaei Botanical Gardens
1800 Dixboror Road
Ann Arbor, MI 48105

MINNESOTA

MINNESOTA NATIVE PLANT
SOCIETY
1445 Gortner Avenue
220 Biological Science
Center
University of Minnesota
St. Paul, MN 55108

MISSISSIPPI

MISSISSIPPI NATIVE PLANT
SOCIETY
PO Box 2151
Starkville, MS 39759

MISSOURI

MISSOURI NATIVE PLANT
SOCIETY
PO Box 176, Dept. of
Natural Resources
Jefferson City, MO 63102

MONTANA

MONTANA NATIVE PLANT
SOCIETY
PO Box 992
Bozeman, MT 59771
(406) 587-0120

NEBRASKA

PRAIRIE/PLAINS RESOURCE
INSTITUTE
1307 L Street
Aurora, NE 68818
(402) 694-5535

NEVADA

NORTHERN NEVADA NATIVE
PLANT SOCIETY
PO Box 8965
Reno, NV 89507

NEW JERSEY

NEW JERSEY NATIVE PLANT
SOCIETY
Frelinghuysen Aboretum
PO Box 1295 R
Morristown, NJ 07962-1295

NEW MEXICO

NATIVE PLANT SOCIETY OF
NEW MEXICO
443 Live Oak Loop NE
Albuquerque, NM 87122

NEW YORK

THE MOHONK PRESERVE,
INC.
Mohonk Lake
New Paltz, NY 12561
(914) 255-0919

TORREY BOTANICAL CLUB
New York Botanical Garden
200th Street and Southern
Boulevard
Bronx, NY 10458

NORTH CAROLINA

NORTH CAROLINA
WILDFLOWER PRESERVATION
SOCIETY
c/o The North Carolina
Botanical Garden, CB#3375
UNC-CH
Chapel Hill, NC 27599-3375

OHIO

OHIO NATIVE PLANT
SOCIETY
6 Louise Drive
Chagrin Falls, OH 44022

OKLAHOMA

OKLAHOMA NATIVE PLANT
SOCIETY
2435 S. Peoria Avenue
Tulsa, OK 74114
(918) 749-6401

OREGON

NATIVE PLANT SOCIETY
OF OREGON
2584 NW Savier Street
Portland, OR 97210

PENNSYLVANIA

PENNSYLVANIA NATIVE
PLANT SOCIETY
1806 Commonwealth
Building
316 Fourth Avenue
Pittsburgh, PA 15222

RHODE ISLAND

RHODE ISLAND WILD PLANT
SOCIETY
12 Sanderson Road
Smithfield, RI 02917

SOUTH CAROLINA

SOUTHERN APPALACHIAN
BOTANICAL CLUB
Department of Biological
Sciences
University of South
Carolina
Columbia, SC 29208

WILDFLOWER ALLIANCE OF
SOUTH CAROLINA
PO Box 12181
Columbia, SC 29211
(803) 799-6889

SOUTH DAKOTA

GREAT PLAINS BOTANICAL
SOCIETY
PO Box 461
Hot Springs, SD 57747-0461
(605) 745-3397

TENNESSEE

NATIVE NOTES
c/o Bluebird Nursery
Route 2, Box 550
Heiskell, TN 37754
(615) 457-7676
Quarterly publication

**TENNESSEE NATIVE PLANT
SOCIETY**
Dept. of Botany
University of Tennessee
Knoxville, TN 37996-1100
(615) 974-2256

TEXAS

**NATIVE PLANT SOCIETY
OF TEXAS**
PO Box 891
Georgetown, TX 78627
(512) 863-7794

UTAH

**UTAH NATIVE PLANT
SOCIETY**
3631 South Carolyn Street
Salt Lake City, UT 84106

VIRGINIA

JEFFERSONIA BIOLOGY DEPT.
Bridgewater College
Bridgewater, VA 22812-
2501
*Publication about the native
plants of Virginia*

**VIRGINIA NATIVE PLANT
SOCIETY**
PO Box 844
Annandale, VA 22003

WASHINGTON

**WASHINGTON NATIVE PLANT
SOCIETY**
Dept. of Botany KB-15
University of Washington
Seattle, WA 98195
(206) 543-1942

WISCONSIN

**WILD ONES NATURAL
LANDSCAPING CLUB**
9701 North Lake Drive
Milwaukee, WI 53217
(414) 352-0734

WYOMING

**WYOMING NATIVE PLANT
SOCIETY**
PO Box 1471
Cheyenne, WY 82003

NATIONAL
ORGANIZATIONS

**CENTER FOR PLANT
CONSERVATION**
PO Box 299
St. Louis, MO 63166-0299
(314) 577-9450 (at Missouri
Botanical Garden)

**CONSERVATION
INTERNATIONAL**
1015 18th Street NW, Suite
1000
Washington, DC 20036
(202) 429-5660

**ENVIRONMENTAL CONCERN,
INC.**
210 West Chew Avenue
PO Box P
St. Michaels, MD 21663
(301) 745-9620

**NATIONAL WILDFLOWER
RESEARCH CENTER**
2600 FM 973 N
Austin, TX 78725-4201
(512) 929-3600

THE NATURE CONSERVANCY
1815 North Lynn Street
Arlington, VA 22209
(703) 841-5300; *for information on regional chapters call*
(703) 247-3724

**SOCIETY FOR ECOLOGICAL
RESTORATION**
Madison Arboretum
University of Wisconsin
1207 Seminole Highway
Madison, WI 53711
(608) 262-9547
*Publishes restoration and
management notes*

**CANADIAN PRAIRIE LILY
SOCIETY**
c/o A.D. Delahay
RR 5
Saskatoon, Sask., Canada
S7K 3J8

**CANADIAN WILDFLOWER
SOCIETY**
75 Ternhill Crescent
North York, Ont., Canada
M1L 3H8

PLACES TO
VISIT

There are still a few places
where one can find a bit of
what North America was
like in the years before European settlement. Some of
these are hard to get to, in
Alaska, for instance. However, every year, millions of
Americans flock to our national parks just to experience nature "in the raw." Of
course, nature never had
roads, or gift shops and
crowds. But, it is surpris-
ingly easy to forget all that,
and to feel exhilarated when
you are in one of these magnificent natural sanctuaries.

Habitat gardeners will find
as much inspiration from visiting public gardens that feature native-plant displays. Be
sure to call or write before
you plan to visit.

ALABAMA

**UNIVERSITY OF ALABAMA
ARBORETUM**
Department of Biology
PO Box 1927
(205) 553-3278
University, AL 35486
Dedicated to Alabama's natives

ARIZONA

**THE ARBORETUM AT
FLAGSTAFF**
PO Box 670, South Woody
Mountain Road
Flagstaff, AZ 86002
(602) 774-1441
*A collection of plants of the dry,
high elevations of the West*

**THE ARIZONA–SONORA
DESERT MUSEUM**
2021 North Kinney Road
Tucson, AZ 85743
(602) 883-1380
*An environment for the
understanding of desert ecology*

DESERT BOTANICAL GARDEN
1201 North Galvin Parkway
Phoenix, AZ 85008
(602) 941-1217
*A natural setting for the study
of desert plants*

CALIFORNIA

THE LIVING DESERT
47-900 Portola Avenue
Palm Desert, CA 92260
(619) 346-5694
Colorado Desert habitat

**MUIR WOODS NATIONAL
MONUMENT**
Mill Valley, CA 94941
(415) 388-2595
*Promotes the preservation and
defense of the redwood forest*

**RANCHO SANTA ANA
BOTANIC GARDEN**
1500 North College Avenue
Claremont, CA 91711
(714) 626-1917
*A center for the preservation of
California's native plants*

**SANTA BARBARA
BOTANIC GARDEN**
1212 Mission Canyon Road
Santa Barbara, CA 93105
(805) 682-4726
*Features a home demonstration
garden for dry conditions*

**STRYBING ARBORETUM &
BOTANICAL GARDENS**
9th Avenue at Lincoln Way
San Francisco, CA 94122
(415) 661-1316
*Visit the Arthur L. Menzies
Memorial Garden*

**THE THEODORE PAYNE
FOUNDATION FOR
WILDFLOWERS AND NATIVE
PLANTS, INC.**
10459 Tuxford Street
Sun Valley, CA 91352
(818) 768-1802
*Preserves California native
plants; 21-acre nursery*

COLORADO

DENVER BOTANIC GARDEN
909 York Street
Denver, CO 80206-3799
(303) 331-4000

CONNECTICUT

**CONNECTICUT COLLEGE
ARBORETUM**
Connecticut College
New London, CT 06320
(203) 439-2140
*More than 400 acres of natural
spaces to explore*

DELAWARE

**MT. CUBA CENTER
FOR THE STUDY OF
PIEDMONT FLORÅ**
Box 3570, Barley Mill Road
Greenville, DE 19807-0570
(302) 239-4244
*Privately owned; visit by
appointment only*

DISTRICT OF COLUMBIA

KENILWORTH AQUATIC GARDENS
Anacostia Avenue and Douglass Street, NE
Washington, DC 20020
(202) 426-6905
The last remaining pristine marshland in the D.C. region

GEORGIA

ATLANTA HISTORICAL SOCIETY
3101 Andrews Drive, NW
Atlanta, GA 30305
(404) 261-1837
Has a native-plant garden

FERNBANK SCIENCE CENTER
156 Heaton Park Drive
Atlanta, GA 30307
(404) 378-4311
Facilities include a 65-acre grounds with nature trails

HAWAII

HAWAII PLANT CONSERVATION CENTER NATIONAL TROPICAL BOTANICAL GARDEN
PO Box 340
Lawai, HI 96765
(808) 332-7324
Preserves and propagates native Hawaiian plants

WAIMEA ARBORETUM AND BOTANICAL GARDENS
59-864 Kamehameha Highway
Haleiwa, Oahu, HI 96712
(808) 638-8655
Stewardship of more than 300 endangered plants

ILLINOIS

THE CHICAGO BOTANIC GARDEN
PO Box 400
Glencoe, IL 60022-0400
(708) 835-5440
Features a prairie home demonstration garden

INDIANA

HAYES REGIONAL ARBORETUM
801 Elks Road
Richmond, IN 47374
(317) 962-3745
Features native woody plants of the Whitewater Valley

IOWA

BICKELHAUPT ARBORETUM
340 South 14th Street
Clinton, IA 52732
(319) 242-4771
An annual prairie burn is an event for the public

KANSAS

THE DYCK ARBORETUM OF THE PLAINS
HESSTON COLLEGE
PO Box 3000
Hesston, KS 67062
(316) 327-8127
Re-creations of the major native plant communities of Kansas

LOUISIANA

LOUISIANA NATURE AND SCIENCE CENTER
PO Box 870610
New Orleans, LA 70187-0610
(504) 246-5672
Environmental education center with an 86-acre woodland

MASSACHUSETTS

THE ARNOLD ARBORETUM OF HARVARD UNIVERSITY
125 Arborway
Jamaica Plain, MA 02130
(617) 524-1718
One of the country's largest collections of woody plants

THE GARDEN IN THE WOODS
180 Hemenway Road
Framingham, MA 01701-2699
(617) 877-7630
Natural gardens, featuring either all-natives or some natives

TOWER HILL BOTANIC GARDEN
30 Tower Hill Road
Boylston, MA 01505
(508) 869-6111
Woodland, grasslands, and wetland plant communities

MINNESOTA

ELOISE BUTLER WILDFLOWER GARDEN AND BIRD SANCTUARY
Contact: The Friends of the Wild Garden, Inc.
PO Box 11592
Minneapolis, MN 55412
Habitats; woodland, bog/ swamp, upland, prairie

MISSISSIPPI

THE CROSBY ARBORETUM
3702 Hardy Street
Hattiesburg, MS 39402-1597
(601) 261-3137
Native flora of the Pearl River drainage basin

MISSOURI

THE MISSOURI BOTANICAL GARDEN
PO Box 299
St. Louis, MO 63166-0299
(314) 577-5100
New home for the Center for Plant Conservation

THE SHAW ARBORETUM
PO Box 38
Gray Summit, MO 63039
(314) 742-3512
Ongoing restoration of tallgrass prairie habitat

NEBRASKA

NEBRASKA STATEWIDE ARBORETUM
University of Nebraska
Lincoln, NE 68583-0823
(402) 472-2971
Forty-four affiliated arboretums statewide

NEW JERSEY

THE CROSS ESTATE
U.S. Dept. of Interior
National Park Service
Morristown National Historical Park
Washington Place
Morristown, NJ 07960
(201) 539-2085
Grounds host very substantial native plantings

TOURNE PARK
EMILIE K. HAMMOND WILDFLOWER TRAIL IN BOONTON
c/o Morris County Park Commission
PO Box 1295, 53 East Hanover Avenue
Morristown, NJ 07962-1295
(201) 326-7600
Trail has labeled woodland plants

NEW MEXICO

LIVING DESERT ZOOLOGICAL AND BOTANICAL STATE PARK
PO Box 100, Skyline Drive
Carlsbad, NM 88220
(505) 887-5516
Chihuahuan Desert preserve

NEW YORK

BROOKLYN BOTANIC GARDEN
1000 Washington Avenue
Brooklyn, NY 11225
(718) 622-4433
Native garden with plants representing a 50-mile radius

CORNELL PLANTATIONS
One Plantation Road
Ithaca, NY 14850
(607) 255-3020
An arboretum, botanic garden, and natural areas

NEW YORK BOTANICAL GARDEN
Southern Boulevard
Bronx, NY 10458
(212) 220-8700
Extensive native-plant garden

OLD WESTBURY GARDENS
PO Box 430
Old Westbury, NY 11568
(516) 333-0048
See meadow and ask about integrated pest management

TIFFT NATURE PRESERVE
1200 Fuhrmann Boulevard
Buffalo, NY 14203
(716) 896-5200
Five and a half miles of trails within a 264-acre park

WAVE HILL
675 West 252nd Street
Bronx, NY 10471
(212) 549-2055
Restored urban forest

NORTH CAROLINA

THE NORTH CAROLINA ARBORETUM
PO Box 6617
Asheville, NC 28816
(704) 665-2492
Approximately 2,000 kinds of native plants

NORTH CAROLINA BOTANICAL GARDEN
University of North Carolina–Chapel Hill
Laurel Hill Road
Chapel Hill, NC 27514
(919) 967-2246
Impressive carnivorous plant collection and native habitats

SARAH P. DUKE GARDENS
Duke University
Durham, NC 27706
(919) 684-3698
Landscaped garden of native plants of the Southeast

UNIVERSITY OF NORTH
CAROLINA-CHARLOTTE
BIOLOGY DEPT.
Charlotte, NC 28223
(704) 547-2555
*Visit Van Landingham Glen to
see native plants*

WING HAVEN FOUNDATION
GARDENS AND BIRD
SANCTUARY
248 Ridgewood Avenue
Charlotte, NC 28209
(704) 331-0664
*Formal garden and wooded
areas designed to harbor birds*

OHIO

THE DAWES ARBORETUM
7770 Jacksontown Road SE
Newark, OH 43055
(614) 323-2355
*Native plants including those of
the Ohio prairie*

THE GARDEN CENTER OF
GREATER CLEVELAND
11030 East Boulevard
Cleveland, OH 44106
(216) 721-1600
Visit their wildflower garden

THE HOLDEN ARBORETUM
9500 Sperry Road
Menton, OH 44060-8199
(216) 946-4400
*More than 3,100 acres of
gardens and landscape* `

OREGON

THE BERRY BOTANIC
GARDEN
11505 SW Summerville
Avenue
Portland, OR 97219
(503) 636-4112
*Has a water garden, a fern
garden, and a native-plant trail*

HOYT ARBORETUM
4000 SW Fairview
Boulevard
Portland, OR 97221
(503) 228-8732
*Woods and meadows feature
natives and exotics*

LEACH BOTANICAL GARDEN
6704 SE 122d Avenue
Portland, OR 97236
(503) 761-9503
*Dedicated to the study of native
plants of the Pacific Northwest*

PENNSYLVANIA

BOWMAN'S HILL
WILDFLOWER PRESERVE
PO Box 103
Washington Crossing, PA
18977-0103
(215) 862-2924
For wildflower preservation

THE HENRY FOUNDATION FOR
BOTANICAL RESEARCH
801 Stony Lane
Gladwyne, PA 19035-0007
(215) 525-2037
*Extensive native and rare plant
collection*

JENNINGS ENVIRONMENTAL
EDUCATION CENTER
Dept. of Environmental
Resources
RD 1
Slippery Rock, PA 16057
(412) 794-6011
*A nonprofit conservation
agency, nature trails*

LONGWOOD GARDENS
PO Box 501
Kennett Square, PA 19348-
0501
(215) 388-6741
*Features native plants of the
New Jersey Pine Barrens*

THE TYLER ARBORETUM
515 Painter Road
PO Box 216
Lima, PA 19037
(215) 566-5431
*Twenty miles of trails through
wood and vale*

TENNESSEE

CHEEKWOOD BOTANICAL
GARDENS
Forrest Park Drive
Nashville, TN 37205
(615) 353-2148
*Visit the Howe Garden of
Native Plants*

MEMPHIS BOTANICAL
GARDEN
750 Cherry Road
Memphis, TN 38117-4699
(901) 685-1566
*Native plant collection of the
Southeast*

WARNER PARK NATURE
CENTER
7311 Highway 100
Nashville, TN 37221
(615) 352-6299
*2,665-acre environmental
education center*

TEXAS

HOUSTON ARBORETUM AND
NATURE CENTER
4501 Woodway Drive
Houston, TX 77024
(713) 681-8433
*Preserves and champions the
native plants of Harris County*

THE MERCER ARBORETUM &
BOTANIC GARDENS
22306 Aldine-Westfield
Humble, TX 77338
(713) 443-8731
*214 acres of east Texas piney
woods, and five miles of trails*

THE NATIONAL WILDFLOWER
RESEARCH CENTER
2600 FM 973 N
Austin, TX 78725-4201
(512) 929-3600
*Dedicated exclusively to
preserving and promoting natives*

THE SAN ANTONIO
BOTANICAL CENTER
555 Funston Place
San Antonio, TX 78209
(512) 821-5143
Texas native-plant collection

WILD BASIN WILDERNESS
PRESERVE
PO Box 13455
Austin, TX 78711
(512) 327-7622
*A nonprofit organization for the
preservation of its 227 acres*

UTAH

RED BUTTE GARDENS AND
ARBORETUM
Building 436
University of Utah
Salt Lake City, UT 84112
(801) 581-5322

VIRGINIA

GREEN SPRING FARM PARK
4603 Green Spring Road
Alexandria, VA 22312
(703) 642-5173
Has a native garden

ORLAND E. WHITE
ARBORETUM
PO Box 175
Boyce, VA 26220
(703) 837-1758
*Native and exotic plant
collections*

THE WINKLER BOTANICAL
PRESERVE
4900 Seminary Road
Alexandria, VA 22311
(703) 578-7888
*Representative flora of the
Potomac drainage basin*

WASHINGTON

THE BLOEDEL RESERVE
7571 NE Dolphin Drive
Bambridge Island, WA
98110
(206) 842-7631
*Preserve with informal and
formal gardens*

WISCONSIN

UNIVERSITY OF WISCONSIN
MADISON ARBORETUM
1207 Seminole Highway
Madison, WI 53711
(608) 263-7888
*Prairies, forests, and wetlands;
covers 1,280 acres*

CANADA

THE ARBORETUM
University of Guelph
Guelph, Ontario
Canada N1G 2W1
(519) 824-4120
*Has an extensive collection of
native plants of Ontario*

THE MEMORIAL UNIVERSITY
BOTANICAL GARDEN AT
OXEN POND
Memorial University of
Newfoundland
St. John's, Newfoundland
Canada A1C 5S7
*Habitats and native plants of
Labrador and Newfoundland*

ROYAL BOTANICAL GARDENS
Box 399
Hamilton, Ontario
Canada L8N 3H8
(416) 527-1158
*Fifty miles of nature trails
representing several habitats*

UNIVERSITY OF BRITISH
COLUMBIA BOTANICAL
GARDEN
University of British
Columbia
6501 NW Marine Dr.
Vancouver, British
Columbia
Canada V6T 1W5
(604) 228-3928
*Very large native-plant
collection*

SUGGESTED READING

One of the early things to do when starting a habitat garden is to arm yourself with guidebooks to the flora and fauna of your region. The best of these have color photographs or drawings. Look at a few of the available ones and compare them to see which ones have the best pictures and most information. Check the Latin and common names of the plants. Any guide that fails to give the generic or scientific names of plants is practically worthless, or suspect at best. In the case of plants, thorough handbooks describe what habitat the plant hails from, the season of its bloom, general height, color of blossoms, shape of leaves, and kindred species. Other helpful information might be wildlife value, for example, and inhabitants that share the botanical community with the plant under investigation. Native-plant catalogs often have useful growing information, as well.

Listed below are some of the many books used in the preparation of this volume. In addition to botanical and horticultural texts, there is a wealth of American nature writing that can be helpful, entertaining, as well as enlightening.

Amos, Stephen H., and William H. Amos. *Atlantic & Gulf Coasts. The Audubon Society Nature Guides.* New York: Alfred A. Knopf, 1985.

Art, Henry W. *The Wildflower Gardener's Guide: California, Desert Southwest, and Northern Mexico Edition.* Pownal, Vt.: A Garden Way Publishing Book, Storey Communications, 1990.

———. *The Wildflower Gardener's Guide: Midwest, Great Plains, and Canadian Prairies Edition.* Pownal, Vt.: A Garden Way Publishing Book, Storey Communications, 1991.

———. *The Wildflower Gardener's Guide: Northeast, Mid-Atlantic, Great Lakes, and Eastern Canada Edition.* Pownal, Vt.: A Garden Way Publishing Book, Storey Communications, 1987.

Bailey, Liberty Hyde. *Hortus Third: A Concise Dictionary of Plants Cultivated in the United States and Canada.* Revised and expanded by the staff of the Liberty Hyde Bailey Hortorium, Cornell University, New York: Macmillan, 1976.

Bir, Richard E. *Growing and Propagating Showy Native Woody Plants.* Chapel Hill: The University of North Carolina Press, 1992.

Blumer, Karen. *Long Island Native Plants for Landscaping: A Source Book.* New York: Growing Wild Publications, 1990.

Brown, Lauren. *Grasses, An Identification Guide.* Boston: Houghton Mifflin, 1979.

———. *Grasslands, The Audubon Society Nature Guides.* New York: Alfred A. Knopf, 1985.

Coombs, Allen J. *Dictionary of Plant Names.* Portland, Oreg.: Timber Press, 1985.

Curtis, Will C., revised by William E. Brumback. *Propagation of Wildflowers.* Framingham, Mass.: New England Wild Flower Society, 1986.

Druse, Ken. *Burpee American Gardening Series: Flowering Shrubs.* New York: Prentice Hall, 1992.

———. *Burpee American Gardening Series: Water Gardening.* New York: Prentice Hall, 1993.

———. *The Natural Garden.* New York: Clarkson N. Potter, 1989.

———. *The Natural Shade Garden.* New York: Clarkson N. Potter, 1992.

Ellefson, Connie, Tom Stephens, and Doug Welsh. *Xeriscape Gardening: Water Conservation for the American Landscape.* New York: Macmillan, 1992.

Finlayson, Max, and Michael Moser. *Wetlands.* New York: Facts on File, 1991.

Hightshoe, Gary L. *Native Trees, Shrubs, and Vines for Urban and Rural America.* New York: Van Nostrand Reinhold, 1988.

Jensen, Jens. *Siftings.* Baltimore: The Johns Hopkins University Press, 1990.

Leopold, Aldo. *A Sand County Almanac.* New York: Ballantine Books, 1966.

Lyon, Thomas J., ed. *This Incomparable Land, A Book of American Nature Writing.* New York: Penguin Books, 1989.

MacMahon, James A. *Deserts, The Audubon Society Nature Guides.* New York: Alfred A. Knopf, 1985.

McConnaughey, Bayard H., and Evelyn McConnaughey. *Pacific Coast, The Audubon Society Nature Guides.* New York: Alfred A. Knopf, 1990.

Marinelli, Janet, ed. *Brooklyn Botanic Garden Record: The Environmental Gardener.* Brooklyn, N.Y.: Brooklyn Botanic Garden, 1992.

———, and Judith D. Zuk, eds. *Brooklyn Botanic Garden Record: Trees, A Gardener's Guide.* Brooklyn, N.Y.: Brooklyn Botanic Garden, 1992.

Middleton, David. *Ancient Forests.* San Francisco: Chronicle Books, 1992.

Mitchell, Alan. *The Trees of North America.* New York: Facts on File, 1987.

National Wildlife Research Center, The. *The National Wildlife Research Center's Wildflower Handbook.* 2nd ed. Austin: Voyageur Press, 1992.

Niehaus, Theodore F., and Charles L. Ripper. *A Field Guide to Pacific State Wildflowers.* Boston: Houghton Mifflin, 1976.

Niering, William A. *Wetlands, The Audubon Society Nature Guides.* New York: Alfred A. Knopf, 1985.

Ogden, Scott. *Gardening Success with Difficult Soils.* Dallas: Taylor Publishing Company, 1992.

Peterson, Lee Allen. *A Field Guide to Edible Wild Plants: Eastern/Central North America.* Boston: Houghton Mifflin, 1977.

Peterson, Roger Tory, and Margaret McKenny. *A Field Guide to Wildflowers.* Boston: Houghton Mifflin, 1968.

Phillips, Harry R. *Growing and Propagating Wildflowers.* Chapel Hill: The University of North Carolina Press, 1985.

Phillips, Judith. *Southwestern Landscaping with Native Plants.* Sante Fe: Museum of New Mexico Press, 1987.

Phillips, Roger, and Martyn Rix. *A Random House Book of Shrubs.* New York: Random House, 1989.

Runkel, Sylvan T., and Dean M. Roosa. *Wildflowers of the Tallgrass Prairie.* Ames, Iowa: Iowa State University Press, 1989.

Smith, Robert I., and Beatrice S. Smith. *The Prairie Garden.* Madison: The University of Wisconsin Press, 1980.

Sunset Books and Sunset Magazines, Editors of. *Sunset Western Garden Book.* Menlo Park, Calif.: Lane Publishing, 1988.

Sutton, Ann, and Myron Sutton. *Eastern Forests, The Audubon Society Nature Guides.* New York: Alfred A. Knopf, 1985.

Wasowsky, Sally, and Andy Wasowsky. *Native Texas Plants.* Houston: Gulf Publishing, 1988.

Whitney, Stephen. *Western Forests, The Audubon Society Nature Guides.* New York: Alfred A. Knopf, 1985.

Wyman, Donald. *Wyman's Gardening Encyclopedia.* New York: Macmillan, 1971.

INDEX